Models of History Teaching
in the Secondary School

Oxford studies in education

Models of History Teaching in the Secondary School

Brian Garvey

Mary Krug

Oxford University Press 1977

Oxford University Press, Walton Street, Oxford OX2 6DP

Oxford   London   Glasgow   New York
Toronto   Melbourne   Wellington   Cape Town
Ibadan   Nairobi   Dar es Salaam   Lusaka   Addis Ababa
Kuala Lumpur   Singapore   Jakarta   Hong Kong   Tokyo
Delhi   Bombay   Calcutta   Madras   Karachi

ISBN 0 19 919061 5

Printed in Great Britain by
Visual Art Productions Ltd.
Kidlington, Oxford

Contents

Preface

The training of secondary school teachers has undergone changes in the last ten years similar to those in other sections of formal education. Not only has technical gadgetry, including the use of closed-circuit television, enlarged the options open to a teacher-educator, the system of training in teaching skills has been reconsidered and largely replanned as those skills have been defined and categorized more precisely. The introduction of micro-teaching techniques in particular has made the teaching of 'methods' more practical and profitable. Micro-teaching involves a system in which a student is required to instruct a small group of pupils for a short period of time, with a limited but very definite teaching objective. Many of the skills of teaching can thus be practised bit by bit, before the student attempts to synthesize them in a regular forty-minute practice lesson.

This book has grown out of a course in history teaching methods given at the University of Zambia which makes considerable use of micro-teaching techniques. The basic strategies of teaching history, determined by the principal or central resource, are practised in short teaching exercises before being attempted in regular teaching hours. These strategies are studied and analysed in demonstrations and are related both to an understanding of history as a discipline and to the educational needs of adolescents in secondary schools. This book is written for teachers and students in education colleges and departments for specific training in the skills of teaching history.

We are of course well aware that many of the insights and ideas in the following pages are derived not only from our own reading and teaching experience, but from casual conversations with friends and colleagues. We would like in this regard to express our gratitude to Tom Black, Godfrey Dalton, Beryl Steel, Philip Thompson, Romilly Turton, and to all our former students in

ED 322 and ED 422 at the University of Zambia, and the
schoolboys of Kabulonga Boys' School and Matero Boys' School
who have assisted with our demonstrations and experiments. We
wish also to express our gratitude to the Research and Higher
Degrees Committee of the University of Zambia for research funds
which helped to further our studies of history teaching in 1974
and 1975.

Lusaka, Zambia
September 1975

Introduction: History and learning in the secondary school

This book has been written for the benefit of future teachers of history in secondary schools. Most students of education who read this sort of book will either have already completed their tertiary studies in history as a subject (if for example they have taken a degree), or they will be well advanced in post-secondary history (if they are taking academic and professional courses concurrently in a degree or training programme). Before being introduced to the various ways in which individual disciplines can be taught in a classroom, such students should have read some of the relevant literature in the fields of educational philosophy and psychology. They will have discovered therefore that teaching is not an exercise which a teacher performs in front of a roomful of pupils, but is really an ancillary activity by which one person helps others to learn. They will also have begun to realize that the many ways in which pupils learn are affected not only by the sort of teaching to which they are subjected, but also by the pupils' own intellectual and emotional development. So the teacher has to subordinate many of his own interests and enthusiasms to the learning needs of his pupils, and to adapt the objectives of his lessons to the developmental stages through which his pupils pass.

If teaching history means helping someone else to learn the subject, then it would be as well for us to ask just what the learning of history entails before we examine the strategies and techniques by which the teacher can assist that learning. Unfortunately for the purposes of clear definition, history as a concept is very broad. The subject can encompass almost every aspect of a community's past, and inevitably involves a wide range of intellectual and imaginative

1

activities. Even the phrase 'studying history' can mean different things to different people. If these things are summarized and placed in a hierarchy of intellectual difficulty and professional value, studying history can mean:

a)   to acquire knowledge of historical facts;

b)   to gain an understanding or appreciation of past events or periods or people;

c)   to acquire the ability to evaluate and criticize historical writing;

d)   to learn the techniques of historical research;

e)   to learn how to write history.

In the following paragraphs we will examine each of these aspects of historical study and comment on their relevance to the situation in the average secondary school.

Historical facts

Until fairly recently the major emphasis in a good deal of secondary school history learning has been laid on the memorization of a store of historical facts, to be repeated with the greatest possible accuracy during examinations or tests. While it is still true that to know history one has to learn what happened in the past, the primacy of purely factual knowledge has been challenged from two different directions:

1   In nearly all academic disciplines the modern student is faced with more facts than he can reasonably be expected to memorize or master. Sometimes this problem is referred to as an 'information explosion'. In the natural sciences, in new areas of language study and to some degree in the social sciences, the total amount of useful information has already surpassed what a single human being can be expected to control. The use of the computer, while assisting human intellects to store and retrieve almost unlimited amounts of factual knowledge, has added to the problem by providing quicker ways of processing the old and of discovering still more new facts. So the experts in broad areas are rapidly disappearing, and expertise even in very

narrow fields of knowledge is becoming more and more difficult to acquire.

This problem has of course always been inherent in the study of history. The human past has always been too wide for any one man or woman to cover adequately. But while it has always been accepted that every human community has a history that is worth investigating by someone, in secondary schools and in many colleges and universities students have frequently been encouraged to limit their attention to the past, and often only the political past, of their own national grouping and its immediate neighbours. This custom has been found wanting in recent years. The growth of the social sciences, especially economics and sociology, has caused historians to look at more than just the political activities of the past and has persuaded them that when seen in isolation those political activities cannot be fully understood. Furthermore, the growth of communications of all kinds in the modern world, and the increasing contact between peoples either through migration or travel or even indirectly through television and other media, has caused educationists to have misgivings about the value of studying the history of one small community and its immediate surroundings. Educated people need to know more than their grandparents did about other parts of the globe and other cultures. To give an historical dimension to such knowledge means enlarging the areas covered by the traditional syllabus. But in this context of a wider world, it is obviously quite impossible to provide a syllabus which will cover 'all the facts'. Selection is necessary, but along with selection must go some training in those skills which will enable pupils both to use the selected knowledge they have acquired in a valid and intelligent way, and also enable them to acquire new knowledge without having to depend upon a teacher.

2 But while the number of historical facts is constantly increasing as researchers examine new areas of study or devise new ways of analysing old ones, the concept of an historical fact has also been undergoing development, both in the academic world and in schools.

It is ironic that the nineteenth-century methods of using the newly available archival sources in order to establish historical facts precisely and absolutely should have led to the discovery that comparatively few of the past activities of people are factually definable. Historians must discover their facts from evidence. Where there is little first-hand evidence the facts tend to remain undisputed, but where, as in modern history, evidence is prolific, it often becomes clear that no single item of primary source material will give a complete objective picture of even one fact. There is little doubt about how and why Julius Caesar was assassinated. Historians have no eye-witness descriptions to study and must rely wholly upon accounts given by ancient historians such as Plutarch and Suetonius. The murder of John F. Kennedy was seen by thousands, witnesses have testified, and experts have analysed the evidence. But few people are convinced that we know the whole or the real story. What the facts were seems to depend largely upon one's interpretation of the sources, and, as interpretations change, the facts in history books can change as well.

All this has had some influence on the way historical facts are regarded in the secondary school classroom. But the introduction of non-political history has also changed teachers' ideas about what sort of facts are suitable for school study. Political events are important in so far as they have influenced the lives of people or the development of human communities. It is obviously just as important therefore to know how people's lives were influenced or what happened to their societies. And this introduces another type of historical fact: How did people live in certain ages? How were their economic, religious, or cultural lives organized? These facts may not relate just to one known historical person or group, but can be more general, deriving information from a variety of examples and creating a general picture. Interpretation is again very important in this activity, and the resulting 'facts' are not as easily defensible as the result of an experiment in the physical sciences. But such facts form part of the basic structure of history as a subject and should therefore be studied and learned in the secondary school.

Understanding the past

Good history teaching has never limited itself to factual knowledge, and pupils in the past as in the present have been required to obtain an imaginative and analytical understanding of the development of historical events. In fact history teachers have often maintained that the educational value of their subject is related to the skills of historical understanding, which the adolescent can apply in every-day life to other areas of intellectual concern such as the appreciation of current society, culture, or politics. Since this may also be true of many other subjects, it is worth asking just what intellectual skills are proper to the discipline of history, and are not shared by other sciences. We can recognize that the historian and the history student have a definite mental bent: an attitude of mind formed by their education which causes them to examine issues—even issues outside their subject—in a different way from a sociologist or a student of literature. What specific emphases in the intellectual formation of the historian have led to this distinct mentality or *gestalt*? We can readily identify at least three of them: firstly, an interest in time and its use in identifying and analysing change or development; secondly, a strong pictorial and empathetic imagination; and thirdly, an understanding that the past (and the present) can only be understood fully if all its facets are studied, and the interaction of a variety of factors in one or several human lives is not merely analysed but is also seen as a whole.

1   The development of an historical time sense must include both the mastery of the basic concepts of time and their use in historical argument. By secondary school age pupils have acquired a considerable understanding of time and its uses: they can calculate the day of the week or the hour of the day; they are even old enough to think of their own past in terms of years. At the simplest level they need through secondary school instruc-tion to extend their imaginative understanding of time into the decades and centuries of the past. But besides understanding about time they need to learn how to use it. An historian builds his explanation of the past—his argument—around the chronology which he or others have been able to establish. His first, often subconscious, act in trying to identify a relationship between events is to put them into their context of time. This act can be subconscious because it has been practised over years of training, beginning before secondary schooling and continuing in all tertiary historical studies. If a pupil has acquired the habit

of forming a time pattern out of events then his secondary education has helped him to establish one of the basic dimensions of an historian's mental framework or *gestalt.*

2 The controlled use of the imagination is another mental activity essential to an historian's objective of understanding the past. Like every scientist, the historian tries to create a rational explanation for the data provided by his evidence. Unlike other scientists, he does not witness his data; he does not see a reaction as a chemist sees it in a laboratory or as an anthropologist sees it in a human confrontation. Before analysing it, the historian has to re-create the data from his evidence, and this act of re-creation, upon which all else depends, takes place in his imagination.

Few writers on the discipline of history have attempted to analyse the concept of historical imagination. The most famous of those who made the attempt was probably R.G. Collingwood, himself a practising historian as well as a professional philosopher. Collingwood examined imagination in historical writing and drew a distinction between the 'ornamental' use of imagination (whereby a writer vividly clothes an event in interesting detail) and the 'a priori' or (more helpfully) 'structural' imagination (whereby the researcher fills the gaps in his narrative left by lack of evidence by using his own powers of imaginative reasoning).

In the secondary school both of Collingwood's categories may be relevant, but before a pupil can write imaginatively he must learn to *think* with his imagination. This thinking may involve two distinct types of imaginative activity. Pupils need to be able to think *pictorially,* to imagine the detail of what is presented in abstract print, and to imagine with authentic detail the historical reality. But they also need to be able to place themselves *empathetically* in an historical situation, to imagine by feeling as well as by seeing, since the human events they study in history have an emotional as well as a pictorial context. During adolescence imaginative powers are usually sharp, and the task of the history teacher is to enable pupils to control their imaginations, to restrict them to the data presented by the evidence, and to use them in the creation of historical narrative or argument.

3 The process of thinking empathetically, or putting oneself

6

imaginatively in the situation of an historical person or event, should force the student of history to see the past as a whole, even if he is often obliged to study it in parts. History is limited by the amount of evidence which has survived, but the historian has to study all of the surviving sources from every relevant aspect. While it is true that history as a discipline has its specialities—economic history, demographic history, etc.—the mainstream historian is one who has taken every point of view into consideration in his study of a topic. This cannot be done without first categorizing those aspects which are relevant to the data and then analysing the evidence thoroughly from each aspect. But categorization and analysis, while essential, are not the whole story. The historian has to synthesize: he has to fit different viewpoints on the past together, and in doing this he becomes aware of the richness of the whole, as experienced by the historical characters who lived through the events he is studying. Denys Hay specified this imaginative synthesis as one of the elements of history in an often quoted sentence: 'The hallmark of the historically minded person is an itch for the concrete, a desire to get behind the generalizations to the facts on which they are based and to establish an almost physical relationship with the texture of earlier times.' To help pupils understand the texture of history is to help them to become not merely students of history but historically minded.

Critical reading

Most of the reading required of secondary school pupils consists of secondary historical material: the writings of historians who may or may not themselves have studied the primary evidence of the past. When we attempt an evaluation of secondary historical writing we too normally have to do it without studying the evidence at first hand, without that is to say duplicating the historian's own research. There are only two ways in which we can rationally criticize a work of history if we are not as well acquainted with the sources as the author we are studying: we either compare his work to other examples on the same topic, or we examine the interior logic of the book to see whether the argument is rational or the inferences reasonable in view of the quoted evidence.

In secondary schools pupils have sometimes in the past been regarded as empty vessels waiting to be filled with knowledge, or in our discipline, with narrative. Some teachers would hesitate to allow adolescents whose reading of history is not very wide to attempt to evaluate the books that they study. This hesitation would make sense if pupils were to be left to pick up the skills of criticism for themselves. But the task of a teacher is to help pupils to learn, and pupils can learn how to read critically, and how to examine the logic and make meaningful comparisons with other explanations or descriptions. In some ways adolescents can be notoriously critical. While they tend to be extremely biased in favour of the culture of their peers they can be healthily sceptical about that of the previous generation. This critical sense can be used in the learning of history, and through history it can be sharpened into a valuable intellectual tool. It may be argued that even for the adolescent too much scepticism is unhealthy, and that the growing young need the assurance of certainty and solid fact. But it is hard to see how this need can be supplied by a subject such as history: foreign languages or the physical sciences would be more useful in that respect. History can contribute to intellectual development through the honing of a critical ability and its application to academic study.

Historical research

Most historical study, in secondary schools and elsewhere, is concerned with reading history books. But it should be quite clear that reading is not itself history. The word 'history' is derived from a Greek word meaning 'inquiry', a search for the truth. And we seek the truth about past events not in books written by historians but in what the past has left behind: its buildings, monuments, and artefacts, its immense literary debris of published works and private memoranda, personal letters, receipts, bills, etc. This is the evidence out of which history, as a narrative or as explanation, has to be fashioned, and the task of studying this evidence has always been the main occupation of the professional historian. It is a task which requires several precise skills, some of them common to all types of scientific inquiry, others general to historical areas, while yet others belong to very specialized fields. The historian has to examine his data, identifying problems in terms of his narrative or explanation, and develop hypotheses to overcome these problems, just as other researchers in every subject. In specialized studies he must acquire esoteric knowledge, like the calligraphy of the mediaevalist or the uncommon language of the ethnohistorian. In all historical inquiry he must use skills relating to the historical understanding which has been discussed above.

There are many fields of history which do not demand impossibly specialized techniques and which can therefore be investigated by pupils well below post-graduate level. Primary sources can be used for structured classroom study as well as for field projects. If the purpose of the teacher is to enable pupils to understand not just the past but also how we learn about the past, then some work involving an element of real historical investigation is necessary.

Writing history

For the professional historian the activities which have already been described—the understanding of the past, the critical study of other historians, the examination of primary evidence—are means to an end, usually the production of another work of historical explanation. The historian's profession requires that he communicate his knowledge of the past to his contemporaries, and while new ways have been devised for doing this (films, exhibitions, television features) the principal vehicle for such communication remains the history book.

The historian has both to narrate (to tell the story) and to explain. Narration is necessary for it is rare that a story will emerge from reading the primary sources alone. In the act of reconstructing the line of events out of the evidence the author will almost certainly have to make use of Collingwood's structural imagination as he infers from the sources happenings which they do not directly relate. He will also have to use powers of organization and expression, because his narrative has to be convincing to his readers as well as to himself.

Explanation is necessary because the historian's audience lives in the present and will not readily understand the language or the culture of the past. But this is where the principal danger for the writer of history lies: how can one translate the past into the terminology of the present without falsifying it? There is always a temptation to explain the past in terms of the values and knowledge of the present, instead of in those of its own time. Thus Caesar may become a right-wing general, Brutus a vacillating liberal revolutionary, and Octavian a slick political manipulator. The narrative may well convince because it is similar to what we expect to find in the present, but do such categories have any meaning as explanations of what happened in the first century before Christ? The answer of course lies not only in the writing of history but in its understanding: in empathy and a professional fidelity to the evidence seen on its own terms. The writer's problem is to preserve this fidelity while putting the explanation into modern language.

Writing in the secondary school has always been an important element in history learning. Too often it can become a form of subtle plagiarizing, where pupils neither absorb nor understand the model author's approach and feeling for his subject. If writing history demands feeling for the period or topic and fidelity in expressing it, then the tasks which secondary school children are asked to perform need to be carefully graded, so that they move gradually towards more complex skills, and from simple to more refined expressions of what they understand.

Sequencing historical skills in the secondary school

The main activities of the history student have been analysed briefly above, with some suggestion of their place in the educational situation of the secondary school. It remains now to examine that situation in the light of recent developments in the understanding of learning and the planning of curricula, and to ask especially how historical skills should be arranged and taught in the classroom.

In the past a great deal of history teaching was based on the assumption that the major activities of the discipline should be mastered in chronological sequence through the years of schooling and tertiary study. While some form of writing took place at almost every stage, history in the primary school or in junior secondary classes was often limited to facts or simple stories to be memorized but not analysed. The understanding of the past, the development of concepts such as historical causality, and the awakening of a controlled historical imagination was left to the senior secondary forms. Critical understanding was the objective of undergraduate or college studies, while research was usually restricted to the postgraduate years.

While history teaching has not been as stereotyped as this for some years now, there seems to be some support for a gradual progression of historical skills in the theories of developmental psychologists such as Jean Piaget. Piaget's influence on educational theorizing has been considerable over the last forty years, and he is best known for his hypothesis that cognitive development passes through consecutive and well-defined stages, from the 'sensori-motor' activities of small babies to the 'formal operations' or abstract thinking of the young adult. Now anything as complex as a real understanding of the past, as demanded by the discipline of history, has to find its place in the latest of Piaget's developmental stages, and R.N. Hallam in a well-publicized study concluded that for secondary school students of history the final stage of formal thinking was not usually reached until about the age of sixteen. This implied that many Ordinary level history candidates in the General Certificate of Education were not yet capable of understanding the past!

The spiral curriculum

Strangely, since the publication of Hallam's findings, history teaching in schools has become even less consecutive in development than before. Projects used from primary levels upwards have introduced an element of research into classroom learning, and there has also been a positive attempt to apply the principles behind curriculum developments in the natural sciences to history. In the sciences it is admitted frankly that the 'facts' are both so numerous and so subject to revision that to limit secondary school learning to a definite 'body of knowledge' would quickly result in irrelevancy. The stress therefore has moved from 'subject matter' to 'structure': the methods of scientific inquiry, the principles behind the empirical facts, an understanding of the discipline, not just of its data.

Much of the theory behind this type of curriculum development has been devised by another educational psychologist whose work has a special relevance for history. Like Piaget, Jerome Bruner maintains that the human intellect grows through definite stages. He describes them according to the manner in which the child interiorizes (represents) the world around him. He concludes that there are three main phases: that of enactive representation (as babies learn through bodily or sensory activities), that of iconic representation (as children create mental pictures and learn to reason through them), and that of symbolic representation (where adolescents manipulate ideas without mental images, using symbolic systems such as language or numbers). The middle phase of iconic representation is particularly important for history teachers, who will recognize its affinity with historical imagination, a central element of their own discipline.

Bruner has carried his studies of cognitive growth further than the elaboration of a developmental system. He has drawn from his theory principles which relate to the shaping of school curricula. If children do develop through defined stages, it is important that subjects are taught to them in ways which are both acceptable at the stage which children have reached, and also contribute to the refining of their faculties in preparation for the next stage. In applying this principle, Bruner further maintains that the main difficulty for a child in learning what are really adult intellectual subjects lies not so much in the structures of the individual disciplines as in the ways in which these are adapted and presented to the learner. In a famous phrase he asserted that 'any subject can be taught effectively in some intellectually honest form to any child at any stage of development', provided of course that the way in which the subject is presented suits the developmental stage of the individual child.

From this Bruner evolved the idea of the 'spiral curriculum', which indicates a system whereby the structure of a subject is taught as completely as possible at every developmental level, instead of being divided into segments which are taught consecutively over the years of growth. This approach to the possibilities of curriculum adaptation has important repercussions for history. Firstly, it clearly conflicts with the old-fashioned idea that facts are for children, criticism for the undergraduate, and primary evidence solely for post-graduate study. At each level, within the bounds of the type of thinking proper to the stage of development, every aspect of history can be utilized. Secondly, most of a child's secondary school career takes place when iconic thinking is foremost, or when the pupil is moving from iconic to symbolic thought. Bruner has suggested that although the developmental stages are consecutive, they do not wholly replace each other. There is a place for mental images in the intellectual life of adults; indeed satisfactory abstract thinking needs an iconic basis. In the secondary school therefore history can play an important role. Structurally it stands on both levels. The historian does not abandon imaginative thinking when he begins to analyse or evaluate. The imaginative faculty must be active during all his formal or symbolic thinking. History is well suited therefore to develop understanding at the iconic level and to help a pupil use his imagination to develop adult reasoning within an abstract system.

Organizing the skills of history

While our understanding of history can indicate which aspects of the discipline are suitable for secondary school pupils, and Bruner's theories on the stages of thought can help us to adapt these historical activities to the conceptual levels of our charges, the classroom teacher has the problem of identifying the many intellectual skills required in historical study and organizing his work so that children receive a thorough and sequenced grounding in them.

In recent years another important influence on curriculum theory has helped teachers define the skills of their subjects more closely and organize them for systematic teaching. From the experience of training courses for servicemen during the Second World War, and out of the behaviourist theories of psychologists such as J.B. Skinner, a 'systems approach' to curriculum design has been developed in the United States of America, where a whole school of curriculum theorists, following the lead of Ralph Tyler, has worked on problems of secondary and tertiary teaching. One of the most important results of the work of this school has been the *Taxonomy of Educational Objectives* drawn up by Benjamin Bloom, David Krathwohl, and others. The *Taxonomy* is meant to be a classification, with a hierarchical scheme, of the cognitive and affective skills taught in formal instruction. For reasons which need not concern us here, the published *Taxonomy* was divided into two 'domains': the cognitive (thinking) and the affective (feeling). This distinction has been justly criticized, and in history in particular it would be impossible to develop an 'itch for the concrete' or to 'establish an almost physical relationship with the texture of earlier times' unless the intellect were assisted and enriched by the affective powers. However the cognitive domain of the *Taxonomy* does indicate a reasonable sequence of intellectual skills expressed in very general terms:

knowledge;
comprehension (translation, interpretation, extrapolation);
application;
analysis;
synthesis;
evaluation.

To make use of this model hierarchy, the history teacher has to decide where his own specific objectives can fit. What about the historical imagination, with its strong affective element? The importance of imagination in history is of course that it is part of the cognitive process, part of thinking about the past, part of writing about the past. Pictorial imagination can be seen clearly as a form of comprehension: of translation in fact. And empathy is an essential element in historical interpretation: another form of comprehension. The structural imagination is no less obviously part of the process of historical synthesis.

At every stage pupils need to be encouraged to develop their skills of comprehension, analysis, synthesis, and evaluation. It is important that the material studied is suited to the conceptual development of the child, but just as a teacher can cause the main structural activities of history to spiral through the curriculum, so the intellectual skills ought to be repeated frequently as pupils refine their abilities and grow in understanding. Any teacher who wishes to draw up a systematic sequence of the skills he intends to teach can devise a personal taxonomy based on the Bloom model. For the purposes of history teaching in secondary schools we have assumed in this book that the sequence of intellectual teaching skills will run something like this:

knowledge of specific facts;
knowledge of generalizations;
translation from one medium into another;
imagination (pictorial and empathetic),
interpretation;
extrapolation;
application;
analysis;
imaginative reconstruction;
explanatory synthesis;
evaluation.

In the chapters which follow we will suggest how different strategies of classroom history teaching can help pupils to acquire such skills as they learn about what happened in the past.

Further reading

Martin Ballard (ed.), *New movements in the study and teaching of history,* Maurice Temple Smith (London, 1970).

Marc Bloch, *The historian's craft,* Manchester University Press (Manchester, 1954).

Benjamin S. Bloom (ed.), *Taxonomy of educational objectives. Book 1: Cognitive domain,* Longmans, Green (New York, 1956).

Jerome S. Bruner, *The process of education,* Harvard University Press (Cambridge, Mass., 1960).

W. H. Burston, *Principles of history teaching*, second edition, Methuen (London, 1972).

W.H. Burston and D. Thompson (eds.), *Studies in the nature and teaching of history,* Routledge and Kegan Paul (London, 1967).

E.H. Carr, *What is history?* Macmillan (London, 1961).

R.G. Collingwood, *The idea of history,* Oxford University Press (Oxford, 1946).

J.B. Coltham and J. Fines, *Educational objectives for the study of history: a suggested framework,* Historical Association (London, 1971).

G.R. Elton, *The practice of history,* Sydney University Press (Sydney, 1967).

Edwin Fenton, *Teaching the new social studies in secondary schools: an inductive approach,* Holt, Rinehart and Winston (New York, 1966).

H.P.R. Finberg (ed.), *The approach to history: a symposium,* Routledge and Kegan Paul (London, 1962).

Michael Honeybone, 'The development of formal historical thought in schoolchildren', *Teaching History,* vol. II, No. 6 (1971).

G. Kitson Clarke, *The critical historian,* Heinemann (London, 1967).

Mark M. Krug, *History and the social sciences,* Blaisdell (Waltham, Mass., 1967).

Arthur Marwick, *The nature of history,* Macmillan (London, 1970).

Part 1
Models of history teaching

Introduction

Most secondary school history teaching is carried out in rather uninspiring surroundings. The traditionally rectangular classroom often communicates to pupils and teachers alike an atmosphere of carbolic and confinement. One of the greatest problems of the teacher of history is to overcome this atmosphere, to use the classroom in the reconstruction of the drama of the past, to people it imaginatively with characters who now exist only in record, and to help the prisoners of the classroom—the children—develop a sense of the past out of what they can see of a sometimes dismal present.

If the classroom is always the same year in and year out there is no reason why the way it is used should also be monotonous and unvaried. A teacher who wishes to interest his pupils in the subject they are studying must devise a variety of methods of teaching them and a multiformity of activities for them to engage in, and not rely simply on the diversity of topics which have to be treated in the syllabus. Over the years many ways of teaching suitable for the discipline of history have been developed—so many in fact that they would seem to defy rational classification. In this book we have chosen to classify teaching methods by the type of resource upon which they most depend. And among resources we count not only the relics of history and secondary works written about historical subjects, but the talents of the pupils and the expertise of the teacher as well. The history teacher should be able to organize his pupils' learning by the employment and manipulation of the following potential resources:

primary pictorial evidence;
primary written evidence;
other forms of primary evidence;
secondary written sources;
secondary graphic sources;

Part 1: Introduction

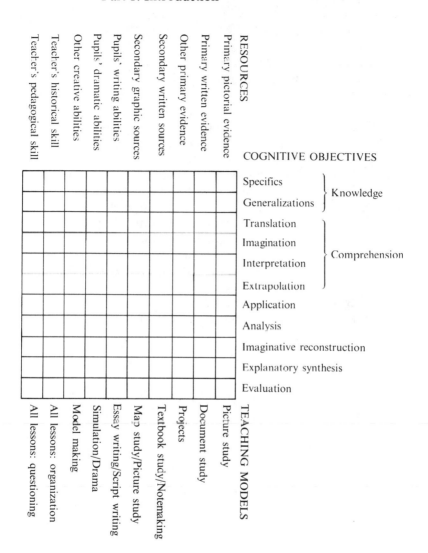

Figure 1   Instructional system for history

19

pupils' dramatic abilities;
pupils' writing abilities;
pupils' other creative abilities;
teacher's historical knowledge;
teacher's pedagogical skill.

In Figure 1 we show how these resources relate to the teaching methods discussed in the rest of this part of the book and how they can be used to further particular cognitive objectives.

The following sections deal with the major methods of organizing pupil learning open to the history teacher. For each, a sample lesson is briefly described and analysed, the rationale of that type of learning is discussed, the many varieties within the category of that method are reviewed, and practical guidance is offered for students attempting that type of teaching for the first time. These method units have been called 'models', not because they describe ideal ways of teaching, but because they do provide a plan for organizing teaching around a central resource, and if put into practice they should produce history lessons of quality and imagination.

1
Picture study

The teacher is moving around the classroom between the groups of pupils who, seated in fours and fives around tables, are examining a series of printed pictures. Each group has a set of five photographs of the stone ruins of Zimbabwe in Central Africa, and under each photograph the teacher has written three questions. The pupils are busy discussing, since each group is supposed to arrive at an agreed answer for each question.

Some of the questions ask for details of the pictures to be translated into words, but many of them include some element of interpretation. *What is the height of the outer wall in this picture?* (Figure 2). The answer is not precisely given in the photograph

Figure 2   Zimbabwe ruins (Spectrum Colour Library)

but it can be deduced from the height of the children standing beside it, provided that some allowance is made for perspective.

Other questions call for some use of the imagination: *How do you think this outer wall was built?* The pupils know that it was built many hundreds of years ago and that the materials available must have been very simple.

'Perhaps they used ladders.'

'What would they have made them from?'

'Wood or rope probably.'

'Did they have strong rope in those days?'

'You can make very strong rope with the inner bark of trees.'

'If they used ropes they might not have needed ladders. They could have hauled the stones up.'

'But how would the builder have got to the top of the wall to lay stones when it was already thirty feet high?'

Do you think the building of the wall required skilled labour? Sometimes the teacher has to intervene to correct a missed direction:

'I think it must have required some skill. What about mixing the mortar?'

'Look again. Can you see any mortar?'

Why do you think such a high outer wall was built?

'Lions!'

'Enemies with spears and arrows!'

'Do lions need a thirty-foot wall? And why should wooden spears need a stone wall six feet thick?'

With nearly half an hour gone and most of the groups discussing the final questions, the teacher calls a halt to the deliberations. Going to the front of the class she conducts a plenary session, asking each group spokesman to report on the agreed answers. Some groups have miscounted or misread the perspective and estimated the outer wall to be seventy feet high. Others produce quite sophisticated reasons for the building of such a defence work. It was a sacred and secret place, so the walls were meant to impress onlookers. It was built by a very ambitious king who wanted the prestige of the most impressive walls in the region. After commenting on the answers and getting general agreement on their merits, the teacher then poses some more difficult problems for the whole class. These buildings date from the iron age of the development of the Bantu societies of the area. What do these ruins tell us of the

community responsible for building them? How were they organized?
What sort of leaders would they have had? What sort of people
were they?

'They were very hard working.'

'No, Miss. They were warriors and had slaves to do the work.'

'They were intelligent. No other group in the area built anything
like that.'

'They must have had strong leaders. . . .'

Gradually the class builds up a series of hypotheses about the
builders of Zimbabwe, their own imaginative reconstruction of a
past society. And the teacher has to tell them that their guesses are
just about as good as anyone else's, for the answers to the riddle of
Zimbabwe are still mainly hypothesis and very little fact.

Lesson objectives

From the point of view of an old-fashioned school inspector or
headmaster this lesson was by no means ideal. It was noisy, especially
towards the end when the plenary discussion was in full swing.
Some of the suggestions were rather wild with little real thought
behind them. On the other hand nobody was day-dreaming, and
the wild guesses were usually recognized as such by the rest of the
class. Did the teacher achieve her objectives? To answer that question
we will have to consult her lesson plan (Figure 3).

Her main purpose was to get her pupils to use their imaginations
in solving historical problems. She realized that the topic under
study presented a very good opportunity for them to exercise an
important skill which would help them to develop true formal
thinking, and at the same time to learn something about historical
study. She wanted to present history as the historians often see it: as
a series of problems. Here was something for her pupils to solve for
which even professional historians have not yet provided a satisfactory
explanation.

In this case the problem appears in Central Africa, where the
strange and beautiful Zimbabwe ruins emerge from the veld. The
problem presented in the photographs and in the questions had
been prepared by the teacher. The essence of the lesson was the
attempt to find the answers rather than the solutions themselves.

Lesson topic : Zimbabwe ruins   *Class* : Third Year
Objectives : Given pictures of the Zimbabwe ruins, pupils
should use their imaginations to solve historical
problems relating to them.
Apparatus : (a) Six sets of five photographs with
questions attached.
(b) Wall map of Rhodesian ruins sites.
Start of lesson : Brief survey by teacher of the discovery
of Zimbabwe ruins and the early ideas
about their origins.

Content	*Method*
Zimbabwe : built 11th -15th century by Bantu ancestors of Shona peoples.	*Activity 1* Group study of pictures and group discussion of questions
Construction :	*Activity 2*
-squared stones piled in rows without mortar	Class discussion of group answers.
-highest walls approx. 30 feet	Summary of findings
-base of walls six feet thick	and agreement on
-methods of building speculative	broad conclusions about
Functions : possibilities:	Zimbabwean society.
-defence	
-protection of animals	
-religion	
-prestige	
Society :	
-evidence of stratification	
-ruling group traders or priests	
-possibility of slave or forced labour.	
- no evidence of foreign cultural or technological influence.	

Conclusion of lesson : Point out that historians have no more
evidence to go on than the ruins themselves and that their
conclusions are just as hypothetical as those of the class.

Figure 3   Lesson plan: Zimbabwe ruins

How were the pupils to proceed? It was not a matter of finding the right page in the right book. There is no answer outside Zimbabwe itself. No literature or valid oral tradition exists for the period when the elliptical ruin was built. Portuguese intervention in the area came later. So the pupils had to look for the answers in the pictures. Any answers produced had then to be checked against the known facts about Zimbabwe. Notice what the pupils had to imagine: How was the wall built? Conjure up a mental picture of men building a wall without modern tools. If your picture includes a shovel or a bricklayer's level, then you must reject it. Imagine men with rough ladders and ropes made out of tree bark. This could have been possible in the technology of the time. Can you *see* them making this wall? What was the purpose of building so high a wall? Now you have to do more than see a picture. You have to imagine thoughts, feelings, ambitions, perhaps fears. If you were a Zimbabwean living eight hundred years ago, what conceivable purpose could you have in building such a monstrous wall there in the valley already protected by your own fortress in the hills. To make this a valid historical exercise such mental pictures need to be analysed and compared with other evidence and the known state of technology in this period, even if much of what we know is merely negative.

Finally, we must ask what the pupils learned. All this hard imagining and all that noise, did it get them anywhere? Did they gain any knowledge they didn't have before? The pupils themselves were disappointed at the end of the lesson that they had not arrived at any hard facts or any clear solutions to the problem. Many of them had approached the lesson as a sort of competition: 'beat the experts'. They expected their teacher to reveal the right answers at the end of the class. But all that she told them was that many of their guesses were worth roughly as much as the guesses of the historians. There are no 'right' answers to these problems, although there are evidently wrong answers. The pupils were left with a negative solution. They had learned what the problem was, what the evidence was, and what the answer could not possibly be. They had not discovered many hard facts, but they had, although they may not have fully realized it, learned something about history. But the main objective of the lesson had been to make the pupils use their imaginations. This they had certainly done, and in doing so had exercised skills of historical thinking.

Models of History Teaching

Why teach through pictures?

Imaginative learning

'The subject matter of history is human affairs, men in action, things which have happened and how they happened, concrete events fixed in time and place and their grounding in the thoughts and feelings of men.' This quotation from the historian Sir Lewis Namier tells us what we are aiming at when we use pictures to teach history. A journalist looks at his own society, his compatriots and neighbours, in much the same way as Namier looked at history. But because he is part of the world which he studies and describes, the journalist does not have to depend much on his imagination. The historian describes a world and a time different from his own. Without recourse to his imagination he cannot hope to represent them to himself or to unfold them to others.

When an historian tries to reconstruct imaginatively the concrete events grounded in another period and another society he tries to create a picture of the event (using pictorial imagination) or he tries to summon up feelings and thoughts surrounding the event (using sympathetic imagination). More will be said about sympathetic imagination or empathy when we consider simulation as a method of teaching history.

We need to imagine vividly the events of the past if history is going to have any impact, interest, or meaning for the present. The fact that the Soudanic ruler Mansa Musa made a pilgrimage from Mali to Mecca in 1324 will not strike us as significant unless we study the detail and begin to picture it: sixty thousand people in his entourage, eighty camels loaded with gold in heavy leather bags, hundreds of camels with provisions for the men, women, and children as they crossed the Sahara to Cairo. . . . As we learn the details we begin to picture the event; we begin to imagine.

In one respect we always remain like the journalist. We carry with us an interior picture of our own times and our own society. The word 'ruler' of a state or nation will inevitably suggest to us some type of contemporary ruler: a presidential figure, or a constitutional monarch, or the leader of a military junta. When we use the word in the context of the Gupta dynasty of sixth-century India, or the Ming emperors of thirteenth-century China or the king of Asante in early nineteenth-century West Africa, we obviously need to modify our normal image of a ruler. Once again, historical detail has to inform our imagination and we must set our notion of ruler in the physical, social, and political conditions of the time and place we are studying. We have to make an imaginative jump into another era.

Pictures and imagination

If you were asked to imagine the court of the ruler of Hungerdingell forty years after the foundation of the city of Drink you would probably find yourself in difficulties. If you were asked to imagine a Roman centurion at the time of Caesar's invasion of Britain you would have much less difficulty. You have seen pictures of Roman soldiers, even if you may remember them only very hazily. But you have never seen a picture of Hungerdingell and for obvious reasons you probably never will. Moreover, you cannot fit Hungerdingell into any context of place or time. You cannot compare it with a similar society because your memory retains no data in any way connected with this fictitious place.

Our memory bank carries throughout our lives thousands or millions of images which our senses have recorded: things we have seen in real life, in films, or in pictures of many kinds. Our imaginations can make use of these interior records provided that there is some developed retrieval system. This often depends on whether the images have been recorded in a haphazard way, jumbled up as things appear in dreams, or whether they have been analysed or processed in our minds. If we are able to use our imaginations creatively in forming hypotheses to answer historical problems, we need to practise using pictorial data in learning history.

Pictures and mental development

It has already been explained that historical thought has to be developed (as do all other types of human thinking) through stages such as those described by Piaget or Bruner. Strictly speaking, the enactive and concrete (iconic) modes of thinking are only possible when the data, the objects of thought, are present to our physical senses. If we had the opportunity to climb the tower at Zimbabwe, or examine the stone walls with our own eyes, we would be able to learn through these basic modes of representation. But it is unlikely that we will be able to take our pupils to Zimbabwe. We must therefore replace real iconic activities by imagined iconic activities to enable the children to develop an historical way of thinking. This can only be done if real data is presented in a pictorial way to their senses.

Pictures are therefore only a beginning. They help a pupil to build up a record of images which will in turn enable him to imagine scenes from the past more accurately and vividly. But we need to help him to go beyond the images, to go beyond the information given and use his imagination to construct reasonable hypotheses or to solve real if simple historical problems.

Ways of learning through pictures

Pictures and problems

If pictures are to be used seriously in teaching history they should be clearly related to specific problems, even if the problem is as simple as 'What is the wall made of?'

The British writer, R.J. Unstead, has suggested that nowadays too many pictures are used in history lessons. But it is evident from his explanation that what he really means is that too many pictures are misused. They can be plastered over classroom walls or used to fill exercise books and still not contribute to the learning of history because the teacher has not related the picture to the particular topic being studied. Pictures will not help to develop powers of imagination or analysis just by being there. They must be used skilfully under the teacher's guidance.

The use of pictures

In the lesson described above, a set of pictures was used as the focus of a forty-minute lesson. Where an historical topic occurs which lends itself to pictorial treatment, such as the mystery of Zimbabwe, the opportunity should not be missed. But many topics are better taught by other strategies, using pictures as an important aid, but not as the focus. It is often suitable to introduce a new topic with a picture study, letting the pupils learn as much as they can from the visual material before they move into a study of written or oral sources. Pictures can be used during instruction as an illustration. And again it is important not to tell the pupils everything before the picture is produced but to leave them something to discover for themselves. As a follow-up to a lesson or to a series of lessons, pictures can be used to stimulate further inquiry or as a memory aid to reproduce the main lines of an historical sequence.

Picture strategies

Now that the general uses of picture studies have been established it remains for us to look at some of the strategies by which they can be brought into the normal context of history teaching.

Picture workcards for group study   The lesson described at the beginning of this section showed how pictures can be turned into workcards by the addition of written questions. If the cards are intended for group work the teacher must take great care in wording the questions written on the cards to avoid ambiguity and to pose a clear problem for the group to work on. There is little opportunity in a group exercise to correct or modify badly worded questions. It is also very important that some of the questions relate to matters of opinion. The groups must have the opportunity to disagree and therefore to have a serious discussion.

Workcards for individual learning   The set of Zimbabwe pictures need not have been used in a group exercise of course. The teacher could have conducted a discussion with the whole class on the first picture, asking the questions orally and then inviting comments from other pupils on the answers offered. Then, with the method established, the pupils could have continued to work on the other cards individually.

Class use of textbook pictures   Most modern textbooks contain a variety of pictures ranging from original source photographs to artistic impressions. If the pictures are suitable it is important that the teacher should invite the pupils to make use of them. Even where the artistic work is historically faulty, the teacher can often get something of value out of pictures by asking the class to spot an anachronism, criticize a misleading historical impression, or identify the bias in a picture. Homework assignments may involve the interpretation of textbook pictures, a welcome change from routine perhaps in many schools. But in all cases the teacher has to set the question, pose the problem, and show how the picture relates to the historical context.

Wall displays   Many history rooms have the walls (even the ceilings) covered in pictures, yet very little pictorial learning ever seems to be done. Pupils should not always be left to themselves to discover what connection there is between a wall picture and the historical topic the class is currently studying. Figure 4 shows a display which has been prepared with questions relating to the background of the topic the class is studying. It invites pupils to look for something specific in the pictures, not simply to glance at them. The questions have turned an artistic display into a learning sequence.

Filmstrips, slides, etc.   The use of filmstrip or slide projectors in secondary school classrooms is very common and the production by commercial publishers or education authorities of visual aids is increasing. When a picture is projected on to a screen, the image is bound to become the main focus of the lesson. The teacher, however, still has to do the teaching, and it is a good idea to let a pupil manage the projector while he directs the attention of the class to the details and the problems displayed on the screen.

Making pictures   So far we have concentrated on the interpretation of ready made pictures presented to the pupils. There has traditionally been a place in history teaching, especially in junior forms, for the making of pictures. This practice can easily cause a lesson to degenerate from history conducted by a history teacher to 'art' organized without the guidance and expertise of the art teacher. If the making of pictures is to become a part of historical learning it is important that pupils do not simply make them, but that they do something with them when they have made them. Writing accurate captions under a strip of drawings, posing questions for other pupils to answer or even writing a paragraph to express in words what the representation tries to depict in images are examples of the sort of exercise which can help children to learn history while drawing it.

Figure 4   Wall display: photographs and questions

Models of History Teaching

Teacher's guide

1 Select pictures which relate to the historical problems of the subject under study.
2 In making a selection from the pictures available, give greater weight to relevance than to attractiveness.
3 Difficult pictures should not be avoided, but they need to be structured for pupil study by helpful questions.
4 Give pupils an opportunity to interpret pictures for themselves.
5 Pictures on wall displays should be clear, simple, and hung at eye level.
6 Wall displays should be arranged with questions or explanations which invite examination and comment by pupils.

Exercises

1 Make a worksheet with one picture on an historical topic and write five questions which invite the pupil to interpret the event or character by using his powers of imagination.
2 Select a picture on an historical topic and instruct a group of children in a micro-teaching session by getting them to describe the picture and draw the maximum amount of information from it. The work of the group should be guided by your oral questioning.
3 Prepare a lesson in which pictorial material is the main focus and the principal resource. After teaching the lesson, ask yourself to what extent your objectives were achieved.

Further reading

R.J. Unstead, *Teaching history in the junior school*, A.& C. Black (London, 1969).
P.H.J.H. Gosden and D.W. Sylvester, *History for the average child,* Blackwell (Oxford, 1968).
John A. Fairley, *Activity methods in history,* Nelson (London, 1967).

2

Document study

The teacher has just finished asking his fifth-year class some questions on the situation in Turkey at the beginning of the First World War. A wall map of the Middle East has been used in this exercise, and the class has been reminded of the physical extent of the Turkish Empire in 1914 as well as of its inherent weaknesses. Now the teacher distributes to each member of the class three cyclostyled handouts, each of them a copy of a published primary source. The documents reproduce excerpts from the following:

1   British Ambassador McMahon's correspondence with the Arabs in 1915;
2   the Sykes-Picot Agreement of 1916;
3   the Balfour Declaration of 1917.

After allowing the class ten to fifteen minutes to read through the three sheets, the teacher asks for any general comments. This is rather a dull fifth-year group and he does not expect a great response without considerable prompting.

'The documents all promise different things', comments one boy.

'Was it the same government which made all the promises?' asks another.

'No, not quite. Lloyd George replaced Asquith and set up a coalition government in December 1916. But to all intents and purposes it was the same, dominated by the Liberals and of course bound by the agreements made by the previous government.'

The discovery of the discrepancies between the documents seems to have exhausted rather than inspired investigation. So the teacher begins to ask questions of his own.

'Look at the first document. Can anyone summarize what

33

Ambassador McMahon was promising and what he was demanding from the Arabs?' Several attempts are made. 'Now ask yourselves another question. Why should the British in Egypt want to make such wide assurances to the Arabs in 1915?' Several pupils rehearse their knowledge of the strategic deadlock after the Battle of the Marne. One of them gets Lawrence of Arabia into the wrong end of the war, and it has to be pointed out that Lawrence's activities were a consequence rather than a cause of the McMahon correspondence. But eventually they agree that the British must have been thinking of using the Arabs against Turkey.

The class then turns to the Anglo-French agreement and is similarly asked both to summarize its content and to put it into the context of the relations between the Allies in 1916. Lastly the same exercise is done for the Balfour Declaration. Here little is remembered although the position of the Rothschilds in the development of Zionism has been mentioned in a previous period.

'There are two big questions to be asked about all these documents. Firstly: What did the British really want? What aim do these documents show them consistently pursuing?'

'To confuse everybody about the Middle East. . . .'

'They didn't have a consistent purpose. They kept changing their minds. . . .'

'They were probably mainly concerned with winning the war. . . .'

'Good. They wanted to win the war. At the back of most diplomatic manoeuvres during a war there are concerns of strategy, which basically means organizing all one's resources to win the war from the present position. But since the position changed between 1915 and 1917, then the manoeuvres also had to change. The division of the Turkish Empire seemed important in 1915. In 1916 it was important to retain the confidence of the French. And in 1917 Jewish financial and other assistance was considered important. Now, the second question: What did the British really want for the Middle East? Did they have any underlying policy that you can see from these documents? And if they did what was it?'

This is more difficult and answers come very hesitantly.

'The documents show that there was no consistent policy. . . .'

'The only consistent thing is that the Middle East would be taken away from Turkey. . . .'

'Good. The Turkish Empire was to be taken to bits after or even during the war. But you remember that for years the British had been the protectors of Turkey. Why was that?'

'Defence of India . . .'

'To protect the Suez Canal . . .'

'They were suspicious of Russia . . .'

'Well, if the main nineteenth-century policy was to use Turkey, however weak, to protect British interests in Asia, what sort of protection of those interests was going to be guaranteed after the First World War? How did the British see the Turkish "buffer" being replaced after 1918?'

This question produces no response. There seems to be nothing in the documents which applies to the protection of the 'British East'.

'Look at the documents again. They all have one thing in common which we have not yet mentioned. Do you see it? . . . Well, answer me this. Do the documents make it clear that after the war Britain is going to be completely uninvolved in the affairs of the Middle East?'

'No, sir. She is still going to be involved.'

'How? What sort of British involvement is assumed in each of the three arrangements?' And the class draws to an end with a discussion of the possibilities facing Britain after 1918, given the desire to extend her influence into the former Turkish areas in pursuance of the old policy of defending the way to her Far Eastern possessions.

Objectives

The lesson plan (Figure 5) shows how, in the planning stage at least, this lesson was intended to fall into three distinct phases or activities. A period of revision directed to a wall map of the area, a period of individual reading of the cyclostyled material, then a teacher-directed discussion of the documents. A good lesson, if it is going to get the maximum return from pupils for the full forty minutes, needs that sort of division of activities. Here we will concern ourselves with the principal activity: learning from a study and discussion of the documents.

The teacher has written his objectives (Figure 5) in strictly behavioural terms. The pupils have to 'describe', to 'translate',

Lesson plan:
Lesson on British and Middle Eastern interest in First World War.

Resources: (a) Wall map of Middle East in 1914.
        (b) Three cyclostyled documents:
           1. McMahon Correspondence, 1915.
           2. Sykes-Picot Agreement, 1916.
           3. Balfour Declaration, 1917.

Content:
I. Remind pupils (by questioning) of:
        (a) shaky situation in Turkish Empire;
        (b) existence of Zionism.
II. Describe Churchill's plan for Dardanelles invasion and its purposes. Briefly describe events:
        Naval attack, Feb 19 th, 1915,
        Army attack, April 25 th, 1915.
III. Distribute hand-outs. Give time for reading.
IV. Conduct discussion on hand-outs, dealing with
        (a) differences between documents,
        (b) policy behind each: Why make promises to Arabs in 1915? Why make agreement with France in 1916? Why promise to Zionists in 1917?
        (c) Which of the agreements was most likely to be kept?
        (d) What was the British policy throughout all this?
        (e) What was the relation to strategy:
          (i) strategy during the war;
          (ii) traditional strategy of defence of East

Objectives;
1. Pupils should be able to describe the Middle East situation in 1914 with reference to a map of the area.
2. Pupils should be able to translate the contents of three official documents showing British diplomatic manoeuvres on the area.
3. Pupils should be able to induce from the documents the background to British policies on the area.
4. Pupils should be able to interpret the documents by describing their relationship to the historical context.

Figure 5   Lesson plan: documents

and to 'interpret'. The first of these objectives could have been realized in a number of forms of study. They might have obtained their information from a textbook, or listened to an oral exposition from the teacher. In fact they were asked to answer questions about a map and then further questions about documents. Had the teacher wanted to write more complete objectives using existential rather than behavioural terminology, he might have said that the students in working on the map would both exercise their memories and help to establish a visual framework for knowledge required on the topic of the Turkish Empire at the beginning of the First World War. In the document study they would exercise simple powers of understanding and learn to express the stilted language of diplomatic usage in the everyday vernacular. The lesson might have achieved both sets of objectives. The success in behavioural terms of the teacher's objectives will only be known after some suitable test or assignment.

The third objective brings us closer to the heart of history as a teaching subject. To interpret the documents the students had to compare them with knowledge they already had from other sources, to place them in an historical context and to see them as part of an historical development, not merely as isolated classroom exercises. This does not mean that secondary school pupils are expected to be able to define interpretation or describe the activities of an historian in interpreting. They are learning by doing. Their rather sluggish thinking, helped consistently by the teacher's questions, is in itself an exercise in simple historical interpretation. And we ought not to belittle the intellectual activities involved. To deduce policy or the thought or tendencies behind the policies, from the published official communications of a government, is to go well beyond the 'information given'. New information is discovered by comparing the common elements in the three disparate proposals with the traditional policies already known to the pupils. For a professional historian this will be a very preliminary exercise in hypothesis, to be followed up in further reading, checked and cross-examined, and as likely as not finally abandoned. For a fifth former it is an exercise in the essential processes of historical thinking.

Models of History Teaching

Why learn history through documents?

In the development of history as a discipline the rigorous use of primary sources in the construction of historical narratives came rather late into the practice of historians. Similarly, the use of published primary sources in the teaching of history at secondary school level came rather late in the development of history as a school subject. Although the idea was proposed by M.S. Barnes in 1904 and again by M.W. Keatinge in 1910, it was not until after the Second World War when publishers had begun to produce collections of documents, and later packs of primary material, that many teachers were able to make extensive use of primary sources as a teaching resource.

Perhaps the strongest argument for using primary source material in the classroom is the need to teach, as Bruner put it, not just the factual knowledge pertaining to a subject, but its 'structure'. Unlike French or mathematics, history as a school or university subject has no determined sequence of knowledge. But Bruner's concept of the structure of a subject cannot be narrowed to the structure or shape of the content material. If history is considered to have its own method or its own system of study, then it has its own structure. But historians maintain that there is a distinctive historical method, and it is a method not just of researching but of thinking. Students who have been limited in their college or university studies to one subject usually graduate with a mental bent determined by the characteristics of the subject that they have studied. They will read differently from specialists in another discipline, because in reading they place the content of the written passages in a particular intellectual framework, determined by the mental training they have received. For example, when reading a speech by a contemporary politician the literature student might look for style or impact (or the lack of it), the political scientist would consider it in the light of theory, and the history student would place it in its context in time and development. These differences would occur because each student had absorbed the structure of thought proper to his individual discipline.

One cannot learn a particular pattern of thought without practising it. There are of course several ways of practising a mode of thinking. If we read a good monograph, we follow the line of thought. We therefore practise in a vicarious way the thought structures of a professional historian. But secondary pupils do not read monographs. They are usually limited to textbooks in which historical knowledge may be recounted at third hand and which retains often only the most tenuous link with argument derived from evidence. To let pupils examine primary evidence, on the other hand, is to allow them to practise in an elementary way the skills that the historian has to use. It is to teach the structure of the subject by making the pupils act within it.

There is an argument occasionally raised by the more prickly historians against the use (and the misuse) of primary materials in the classroom. It takes years of training to do research. To ask minors, adolescents, to 'research' primary source material is utterly inappropriate and can only result in intellectual disaster. Secondary school teachers will not be too worried by this. They know that the average fifth-year essay (taught by the older methods) is usually in historical terms a disaster: just as English essays tend to be literary abominations or French translations a threat to cordial relations with France. If school exercises are regarded more solemnly than they ought to be, they will always seem disastrous. But such 'disasters' are part of the process of learning. Moreover, in using primary sources in a classroom exercise, the pupil is in no sense 'doing research'. He is guided by a teacher, who has done the research already. He is examining prepared documents which have already been worked over, edited, and published very often with an educational use in mind. But his mind does move, with assistance and no matter how clumsily, through the process of historical discovery; and by such activity he develops the thinking skills of the historian.

There is one interesting element in historical documents as a secondary school history resource. They are usually comparatively easy to understand. Granted, the diplomatic language shown in the examples above is not all that easy. But it is clear and deals with one event at a time. Many other types of historical document: eye-witness accounts, official reports, personal letters, etc. are also usually clear, despite old-fashioned style or wording, simply because they are not imbued with interpretation. When a textbook author writes a narrative he is aware not just of the eye-witness accounts of the events he describes, but also of the interpretations and analyses of countless commentators. All their wisdom is likely to be distilled in his account which becomes more than a mere description by the inclusion in some way of very sophisticated thinking. The primary source on the other hand is much more concrete. It tells the story from one angle and not from a consensus of historical opinion. And once archaic words have been explained, pupils often find it much more congenial both to read and to think about a genuine document than a secondary text. Moreover, because most types of primary source are close to individual experience and expressed in concrete terminology, they tend to stimulate the imagination and help to develop the iconic stage of historical thinking.

Varieties of learning through historical documents

If by 'document' we understand a primary historical source of any kind, then we may consider three distinct types of evidence.

Original historical evidence
This is primary evidence in its original form, including written manuscripts, artefacts, buildings, paintings, and other genuine relics of the past. Much of this sort of material is preserved in museums and archival collections, and can therefore be studied by visits and out-of-school projects.

Photographic reproductions of original evidence
There is now a variety of ways of photographing or photocopying material, so that what we see, if not the original evidence, is a true likeness of it. Manuscripts are easy to reproduce in this way, and they can help to bring an air of reality into a classroom study of a subject. Publishers have been issuing packs of such material for some time now and more recently certain archives and educational bodies have been issuing similar collections. There are difficulties with using published sets of material in the classroom, however. The packs are often expensive and the number which can be realistically purchased for a class necessitates sharing and group work, even though the material might inherently be more suitable

for individual study. Most of the published sets have little or no learning structure, no matter how clear the historical structure is. And teachers with little time for preparation do not have the patience to build a learning process into the material. Lastly, the learning value of a snippet of an illegible document (or one in a strange and foreign tongue) is rather small in comparison with its price. In general, the kits recently produced by museums and departments of education avoid these difficulties and are structured for classroom use.

Printed documents
This category includes both books of documents for school or college use produced by publishing houses, and selections from historical sources mimeographed or written on spirit masters by the teacher. Some of the published versions are aimed at the undergraduate market (e.g. *English historical documents,* Methuen); some have been prepared for use in secondary schools (e.g. *They saw it happen,* Blackwell). Others are produced for the general reader but can be used by teachers for educational purposes. Printed documents may lack the visual impact of photocopied sources but they have the advantages of clarity, comparative cheapness, and a convenient format for classroom use. If they are reproduced by the teacher, it is possible to carry out a little judicious editing.

Primary source material can be used in the classroom in two principal ways:

a)   *As part of a project*   A project in this sense would be an (apparently) unstructured discovery exercise, where pupils are presented with resources and are asked either to solve a given problem or to discover where an historical problem lies and then solve it. It is only apparently unstructured because the teacher, who controls the resources, may by his presentation of them determine the general course the pupils' investigation will have to follow. The main objectives of project work are dealt with in a later section of this book.

b)   *As structured exercises*   The exercise in the lesson described above was 'structured' in the sense that the teacher asked a series of specific questions on the documents in order to lead the pupils to a certain well defined understanding. In that case the questions were orally posed by the teacher. It is possible to write the questions at the foot of a document and leave pupils to answer them in individual or group work. Some published series (e.g. 'Town Life and Improvement in Essex 1730-1906', Essex Record Office Publications, No. 62) have questions attached to the sources they print, but these questions are usually scanty and intended to introduce pupils to further study rather than to organize the scrutiny of the printed document. It is obvious that to pose the questions which will lead to a deeper understanding and interpretation of a primary source the teacher must be able both to interpret the document satisfactorily himself and to organize progressively more demanding questions that will lead the pupils from a simple comprehension of the document to a deeper understanding.

Structured exercises therefore will be pursued in one of three possible ways:

1 *In a teacher-directed lesson*   In this type of lesson the teacher asks the questions orally. But it is necessary to prepare the questions beforehand with just the same care as for written questions.

2 *As a group study exercise*   This is particularly useful if there is something controversial in the document. Disagreements about interpretation may result in beneficial discussion and scrutiny. In this case the document should ideally be issued as a worksheet with printed questions.

3 *As an individual assignment to be done in class time or for homework*   But before the pupils tackle this, they must know what is expected of them. As a homework assignment it may be a welcome alternative to the traditional essay.

Teacher's guide

1 Selection of the document

Here much depends on what is available. For English and American history there are now many sources to choose from. In Asia, Latin America, and Africa there are fewer editions specially prepared for secondary schools, but there is still plenty of published material from which the teacher can make a selection and prepare worksheets. The thing to look for is a piece of primary material which is rich in detail, not something that is necessarily complex or artistic.

2 Preparation of the document

Where a book or file of edited extracts is not being used, the teacher should pay attention to the length of the passage to be reproduced for classroom work. Thirty lines can give enough reading and study material for a forty-minute period. Very often too the teacher will have to take account of the incidence of difficult words, especially in work for junior classes. If there are only a few strange terms they can be left in the passage and explained by the teacher. Where there are more than three or four archaisms (and this is especially important for countries in which pupils study in their second language) the teacher should leave them out, replacing them in the mimeographed version with more familiar expressions. This may detract from the worksheet as an historical document, but it will increase its usefulness as a resource for history learning.

3 Presentation of the document

Primary documents can be used either to introduce a topic or to deepen pupils' understanding of a topic which has already been under discussion. How much introduction one provides for any document will of course depend upon what it is used for. At some stage the pupils will have to place the evidence in its context of time, place, and culture. It is important that they are given the opportunity to do this and are not left with an apparently completed exercise without having seen the document in its full context. If a date cannot reasonably be worked out by internal evidence within the primary source (and that might be a useful question to ask of a document) the worksheet should give the date as well as any other data essential for simple interpretation of the evidence.

Reading the document prior to the analysis of its content can be done quietly by the pupils themselves or aloud by the teacher. If the document is a difficult one, or difficult for the age group, then the teacher should read it aloud before study, to assist through intelligent phrasing the basic comprehension essential for interpretation.

Exercises

1 Select a document for a junior secondary class. Type or write
 out enough of the document to provide study material for a
 forty-minute group activity. Write six to eight questions which
 will lead pupils to comprehend and interpret the document
 according to the level which can be expected of their age range.
2 Select a piece of primary material not more than twenty lines
 long, and by oral questioning get a micro-teaching group to
 interpret the document according to its internal structure.
3 Take an 'O' level syllabus and select a document on some aspect
 of it. Prepare a lesson which will achieve the objectives of comprehension and interpretation. After teaching the lesson, test
 how well it succeeds in terms of the objectives. Give a similar
 test after teaching another lesson by a different strategy and
 compare the results.

Further reading

G.R. Batho, 'Sources' in W.H. Burston and C.W. Green, *Hand-
 book for history teachers,* first edition, Methuen (London, 1962).
Edwin Fenton, *Teaching the new social sciences in secondary
 schools,* Holt, Rinehart & Winston (New York, 1966).
M.M. Krug, *History and the social sciences,* Blaisdell (Waltham,
 Mass., 1967).
Margaret Devitt, *Learning with Jackdaws,* Jackdaw Publications
 (London, 1970).
A.D. Edwards, 'Source material in the classroom', in W.H.
 Burston and C.W. Green, *Handbook for history teachers*, second
 edition, Methuen (London, 1972).
W. Lamont (ed.), *The realities of teaching history—beginnings,*
 Chatto & Windus (London, 1972).

3
Questioning

Before describing any further strategies which can be used in teaching history, we need to look a little more closely at one skill which has a role in all effective methods of teaching: the skill of questioning.

In the previous sections we looked at the way in which pupils can study history from pictures and documents. We saw that the questions posed by the teacher directed the pupils to the problem posed by the evidence, and that on the way to a solution the teacher asked other questions to help pupils think historically about the evidence.

Most strategies of history teaching involve an element of problem-solving. All problems have to be presented in some way by the teacher. Questioning is the teacher's way of presenting problems to the pupils and guiding their thinking towards their solution. But too many classroom questions do not fulfil this function: they ask for memorized information or for guesswork which has not been enlightened by a sequenced study of the evidence. This is a serious failure, for a child's learning and thinking will be determined by the types of questions which a teacher asks. One way in which to overcome the temptation to ask too many 'easy' factual questions is to learn how to classify your own questioning. After micro-teaching and practice lessons examine the types of questions asked and the categories into which they fall. Then you will be able to judge whether you are helping your pupils to develop formal thinking in history or merely to memorize historical facts.

Classifying classroom questions

There are many books on classroom questioning techniques, and
we give a selection below in the 'Further reading' section. Unfortunately there are almost as many methods of classifying questions
as there are books on the subject. Some show a very broad type of
classification, for example:

> closed questions (only one correct answer is expected);
> open questions (there may be more than one correct answer).

Other methods classify according to the type of thinking that is
demanded, for example:

> convergent questions (about specific things in the light of general
> knowledge),
> divergent questions (about general knowledge in the light of
> specific examples).

Those who classify questions according to Bloom's taxonomy
stress the type of thinking that the question evokes: knowledge
(memory), comprehension, application, analysis, synthesis,
evaluation.

We prefer a slightly less rigid classification system based on the
modified taxonomy outlined in the introduction, and to make it
we have analysed the questions actually asked in classroom situations.
Different lists have been made, some longer than others, but in
general they look like this:

> Routine questions: Can you all see the map of the Middle East
> on the board?
> Recall questions: What Empire controlled the Middle East at the
> outbreak of the First World War?
> Comprehension questions: What does Ambassador McMahon
> promise to the Arabs in his letter to the Sheik?
> Interpretation questions: How does McMahon's promise to the
> Arabs relate to the Balfour Declaration?
> Extrapolation questions: What do you think were the real intentions
> of the British Government in regard to the Middle East?
> Invention questions: If you had been the Arab leaders would
> you have trusted the British promises?

Questioning

Evaluation questions: If the British really wanted to gain control of the Middle East, would they not have been wiser to choose either the Arabs or Jews rather than trying to be on both sides of the fence?

You have probably noticed that the commonest type of question in many history lessons is the recall question, but that the last five categories are likely to be of greater value in getting children to think historically. But before we decide what type of question is most suitable for secondary school history lessons we should ask ourselves what types of questions historians ask when they study history. What types of questions are central to the discipline of history? Which questions need to be asked if pupils are to learn the structure of the subject as well as the information required for a given syllabus?

Questioning in history

Historians commonly have to study two types of evidence: primary evidence and secondary writing (the works of historians who have studied the period previously and which contain both their description of the events as they understood them to happen and their evaluation of the evidence upon which they have built their narrative). When they are looking at these two sources for knowledge, historians continually ask questions. In fact, they ask themselves the questions, but it is often said that they 'ask questions of the evidence', because it is from the evidence that they expect to get an answer.

While studying the primary source, historians ask questions on the following aspects:

What does the evidence say? What is it? Do I understand it? Can I picture to myself the scene that it represents? (comprehension questions)

How does the evidence compare with what I know of the historical context? Who are the people referred to and what do I know about them? Who is the writer, and what was his purpose in writing? Seeing that the evidence dates from its own period, how must I correct anachronistic impressions of what it means? (interpretation questions)

What new knowledge can I deduce from this evidence? Is there any new light that it sheds on its historical context? Does it contradict any impression given by other evidence about the general historical context? Can I infer more than the evidence tells me about the historical context? (extrapolation questions)

What is the value of this evidence? Is it trustworthy? If it is how much reliance can I place on it when it contradicts other evidence? (evaluation questions)

Historians do not necessarily ask these categories of question in the precise order given above. They ask many questions and all the categories are represented time and again. They often ask, for instance, if the evidence is trustworthy before bothering to interpret it. In some cases a comparison of the evidence with the context throws doubt on its reliability, so an historian will ask if it is trustworthy because of his interpretation. When studying secondary sources the historian will ask not quite the same questions, but questions that fall into very similar categories:

What is the author saying? What does he mean? (comprehension questions)

How does this statement of the author fit into what I know of the topic or episode? (interpretation questions/comparison questions)

Has this statement changed my understanding of the topic? Can I read between the lines, and infer something beyond what the author has said? (extrapolation questions)

What value do I place upon the statement by the author? Do I accept it entirely or with reservations, or do I reject it altogether? (evaluation questions)

Interpretation of historical evidence (primary source) and interpretation/comparison of a secondary statement are not exactly the same thing. Historical interpretation involves putting the evidence in its historical context and understanding it with reference to its context. A statement by an author may be put in an historical context if the author, say, wrote fifty years or more ago. But normally we put it in the context of our understanding of the topic, an understanding drawn perhaps from reading other authors or from studying the primary evidence.

Questioning in history teaching

When we teach history we try to encourage pupils to make the sort of judgements historians make, to see evidence as historians see it, and to enjoy the discovery of new knowledge that historians hope to enjoy. All of this implies working towards symbolic thinking in history. Whereas the historian usually works alone, relying only on his own skills and the published works of his colleagues, our pupils will have to be guided; they will have to be asked questions to provoke certain types of thinking.

Occasionally the teacher will have to ask questions of a routine nature and questions which ask for recall of previous knowledge. But it must be realized that such questions do not go very far towards developing historical thinking. A teacher who wishes to lead his pupils into the discovery of the problems and solutions offered by historical material should frame questions in categories similar to those of the professional historian. It might be useful to think of the process as a three-way relationship between the teacher, the learner, and the resource. The teacher poses the questions which will guide the learner's thinking about the information presented by the resource, whether it is a picture, a document, a textbook, or a map.

It is important that we examine carefully the different types of questions asked by historians which are appropriate for the history teacher to ask his pupils.

Comprehension questions (What is in the picture? What does the document say?) Here the teacher is asking the pupil to put what he sees or reads into other words. Some writers call this translation, since the reader puts the meaning of the passage into another form, even if it is only another form of words in the same language. In the case of a written resource, the comprehension question may also require the pupil to use his imagination to form a mental picture of what is being described; to come to an understanding of the situation at the iconic level of thought.

Interpretation questions (What is the historical meaning of this picture or piece of writing?) Here the pupil is asked to compare or relate the evidence with his outside knowledge in order to detect its

49

historical significance. Again the imagination may be required in order to create a concrete picture. (What would British 'assistance' to Arab nationalists consist of in 1915?)

Extrapolation questions (What can be concluded from the evidence which is not actually stated?) The pupil, having understood the document and interpreted it in the light of other knowledge, is now asked to draw conclusions from it, to use the document or picture and what it contains to create hypotheses, inferences, and imaginative guesses. He will therefore try to go further than the information derived from the document. (Why would the Bantu of the thirteenth century have wanted to build a wall like that?) The answer to an extrapolation question will be rather different from that to a comprehension or interpretation question. An inference will not be right or wrong, but possible or impossible. There may be several possible answers (to honour some religious belief with a very imposing building; to bring prestige to the ruler who had a lot of slaves and could use them to build something quite unusual). But a faulty reading of the evidence will lead to an answer that is impossible (to prevent the village being bombarded by enemy cannon). Imaginative guessing must rely heavily on accurate observation and interpretation.

Invention questions (What would you have done or thought if you had been in this man's position?) This is a directly imaginative type of question in which the pupil is asked to think himself into an historical situation, using the evidence given to inform his imagination.

Evaluation questions There are two levels of evaluative questions:

a)   Do we trust this piece of writing? Even secondary school classes can be asked to evaluate primary documents in the light of their understanding of the period and the author, but this will not happen frequently. More often pupils will be directed to look for examples of bias in standard text and resource books. (Is the author saying this because he is an Arab or because the evidence will permit no other interpretation?)

b)   How effective was the policy of a ruler or a party or the character of an individual in a given situation; what kind of judgement can we make? Here we reach the realm of opinion, where there are no right or wrong answers, but where we find the substance of much historical writing. Was Louis Riel a courageous crusader for human rights in the early Canadian West, or a power-hungry madman who abused the trust of his Metis and Indian followers? Such questions do not traditionally form part of secondary school activities, but tend to be reserved for undergraduate history essays. There is no reason why teachers should not present them to senior forms as interesting historical problems. But they should not expect pupils to do more than attempt to answer them. The emphasis should be on learning how to assemble evidence to support an argument rather than on finding an answer to an evaluation question.

Sequencing questions

In the first part of this book it was suggested that the teaching of intellectual skills should be sequenced in order to enable pupils to progress from one level of ability to a higher level. Similarly, with the types of question asked in the classroom children need the gradual progression provided by a suitable pedagogical sequence.

Secondary school pupils need to be shown the 'safest' way of asking questions, going from the simple to the more challenging. The sequencing of questions by a teacher is in many respects similar to designing a programme of learning—taking the pupil through all the thought processes necessary to reach a certain level of thinking or amount of knowledge. There are many ways of doing this: on a worksheet, for example. All the comprehension questions can come first, and then the interpretation and then the extrapolation. If there are several different pieces of information on the document to be studied, one can take pupils through all the stages for one aspect, before going back to ask them to 'comprehend' another. The sequencing of questions not only assists the pupil in his process of discovery, it also helps to develop his thinking skill by leading him from one step to the next.

Support questions

Quite often a pupil fails to answer one of the teacher's questions. If a teacher is conducting an oral session, or if he is moving about the room listening to group discussions, he will often be able to support the pupil's thought process with another question, usually of a simpler kind.

The root of a pupil's failure to answer a teacher's question often lies in the fact that some step in the reasoning has been left out. The teacher assumed that something had been fully understood, but for this particular pupil it had not been understood. An interpretation question becomes unanswerable because the pupil has not made the accurate observation/comprehension on which the interpretation must be based:

Teacher: How high is that wall?
Pupil: Seventy feet.
Teacher: Look at the boy standing in front of the wall. How high would you say he is?
Pupil: Perhaps four feet or four feet six.
Teacher: Now, how many rows of stones does he cover?
Pupil: Five, I think.
Teacher: Look again, his feet are not on a level with the bottom stone. Put him up against the wall. How high would his head reach?
Pupil: Up to about the eighth row.
Teacher: So if he is four feet in height and he covers eight rows, how much is each row worth?
Pupil: I see: six inches.
Teacher: Yes, only roughly of course, for not all the rows appear to have the same depth. But in that case how high will the wall be?
Pupil: Only thirty to forty feet. . . .
Teacher: Then how high is the wall altogether?
Pupil: Nearly thirty feet.

Interpretation of a picture means accurate observation of what is in it. The pupil observed inaccurately and he estimated the height (interpreted the height) wrongly. The teacher then had to take him back to the beginning of the observation process and lead him to the interpretation step by step.

It is important in this sort of exercise for the teacher *to allow the pupil to think.* It would be very easy to say that seventy feet is wrong and the correct answer is nearer thirty feet. But this would not have brought the pupil any nearer to being able to interpret that sort of photograph for himself. By the supporting question the teacher has enabled the pupil to get back on the track that would lead to a logical and correct answer.

Exercises

1   Take the worksheet you have prepared on a picture, or any other worksheet of your own making, and classify the questions according to the classification recommended for history teaching above. If there are no questions, or only one question, in any of the first four categories, write two new questions for the categories not represented.

2   Classify the questions you have asked in a micro-teaching exercise on learning from pictures. Did you ask any supporting questions? If you did not, prepare some to support the questions the pupils had difficulty in answering. Did you ask any extrapolation questions? If you did not, prepare some for another session.

3   Try to remember two examples of each of the following categories of question which you asked during your last practice lesson: comprehension, interpretation, extrapolation. If any category was not represented, prepare two questions in that category. If there was any question which your pupils could not answer, prepare supporting questions.

Further reading

Norris M. Sanders, *Classroom questions: what kinds?* Harper and Row (New York, 1966).

Roger T. Cunningham, 'Developing question-asking skills' in James E. Weigand (ed.), *Developing teacher competencies*, Prentice-Hall (New Jersey, 1971).

Elizabeth Hunter, *Encounter in the classroom: new ways of teaching*, Holt, Reinhart and Winston (New York, 1972).

4

Textbook study

The teacher is beginning her lesson:

'Yesterday we looked at the Portuguese in Angola and on the west coast of Africa in general. We reached as far as the official abolition of slavery. Can anyone remember when that was?'

'1836, Miss.'

'Yes. As we said, there was officially to be no slavery in Portuguese possessions after 1836, but as we saw it took much longer for the practice to diminish and eventually disappear. Anyway, today we are going to look at the other side of Africa, the Mozambique area, and see what the Portuguese were up to there. Now first, does anyone remember that name of that inland African kingdom with which the Portuguese were trading from the east coast in the sixteenth century?'

'Sofala.'

'No, not Sofala. That was the coastal town through which the gold from this kingdom passed. Can anyone else have a try?'

After several attempts, the teacher gets an answer resembling the correct name of Mwenemutapa, and she goes on to introduce a new concept to the class.

'Along the Zambezi the Portuguese became interested not only in the trade in gold, but in all sorts of trade and even in settlement. According to the accounts, they established what were known as *prazos* in that area. I will write it on the board. Does anyone know what it means? Right, now if you don't know, what is the best way to find out?'

'Look it up in a dictionary.'

'Well, you just try that. Have you got a pocket dictionary? Look up *prazo* then and be ready to tell the class. Now has anyone else got an idea about where to find the meaning of that word?'

54

'It probably tells you all about them in the textbook.'

'Yes, it probably does. But you don't want to read all through the textbook now. How can you find it quickly in the textbook?'

'Look up the table of contents.'

'That is one place to try. Will you do that for us? Can anyone else suggest another method?'

'The index, Miss.'

'Good, now the rest of you can be looking in the index, to see if you can track down *prazo*. . . . So the dictionary man is ready. Have you found the word?'

'No, Miss. It isn't there.'

'I wonder why that is. Why do you think it isn't there?'

'Perhaps the dictionary is too small.'

'Miss, perhaps because it is a Portuguese word, not an English word.'

'Yes, I think you are right. Perhaps you have been looking in the wrong dictionary. Of course there are sometimes foreign words in English dictionaries too, but they are usually words that are commonly used in English. Now, has anyone had better luck with the textbook?'

'Miss, in the table of contents it says, "The *Prazos* and Missions to Kazembe: Chapter 15" but it does not give the page for chapter 15!'

'Yes, there are textbooks like that. It would have been helpful to have put the page numbers for the chapters in the table of contents. And if you think from the chapter heading that the *prazos* have something to do with the kingdom of Kazembe you will find that you have been misled.'

Eventually the teacher and her class find the correct reference to *prazos* in the textbook, and together read the paragraph which describes them. Certain phrases like 'crown lands' and 'absentee landlords' need a little explanation.

'Now I want you to compare the *prazos* with the other type of settlement we studied in the Angola area, the *sobabas*. You will find them described on page 57. What I would like you to do now is read again the description of *sobabas* on page 57, then read about the *prazos* in the paragraph we have just seen and the two paragraphs which follow it. Write down in your rough books the difference between the two types of settlement . . . .'

The class settles down to some more reading and writing. When everyone seems to have finished reading and has written something, the class is asked for its findings. There is not a great deal to go on in the textbook, but enough to see that *prazos* were estates intended for agricultural development but used in fact for purposes of revenue, while the *sobabas* were areas given to settlers, soldiers, and missionaries, with the income from taxes in mind but in fact used largely to supply slaves for the South American market. That established, the teacher then calls the attention of the class to a map of Portuguese East African activities on another page of the textbook. With the class she discusses the reasons for settlement on the lower Zambezi and finds the area on the map which had trade links with Angola, and to which Portuguese East African interest was drawn at the end of the eighteenth century. The class ends with a homework assignment related to that map: to draw on a tracing of the map the route described in the text as that of Lacerda who visited the Lunda king Mwata Kazembe in 1798.

Objectives

On her lesson plan the teacher had specified the following objectives for the class:

1 The pupils should find out specific information from the textbook.
2 They should remember the definition of *prazos* and be able to distinguish them from the *sobabas* already studied.
3 They should be able to describe on a map the spread of Portuguese influence inland from the East African coast.

The amount of factual knowledge that the class was supposed to acquire was comparatively small. Indeed the teacher could have given a perfectly adequate outline of the *prazo*, its difference from the *sobabas,* and its geographic extent in about ten or fifteen minutes. Instead she spent forty minutes on these few details, because she made the class do most of the finding out for themselves. From her second objective it is clear that the teacher thought that by having to hunt for the definition and to study the differences in the textbook, the class would retain more than if they had merely been told. But she was also anxious that the class should learn where to find information. Her other objectives involve developing the ability to use a common resource such as a textbook, and to relate written paragraphs to a map. This was an early exercise in textbook use for this particular class, and the class was able to judge the faults of the book as a useful resource. Two types of comprehension activity were in fact used on the textbook: the straightforward re-phrasing of the paragraphs to show that the content had been understood, and the translation of the written content on to a map. The teacher guided the first of these activities by linking it to a problem: the difference between the two types of settlement.

It is clear that this lesson has not exhausted the topic of the Zambezi *prazo*. The teacher would no doubt go on to deal with life within those settlements. Time was devoted in this lesson to the acquisition of a particular skill. But the skill and the knowledge gained were intimately linked in the one activity. The teacher did this by giving factual problems to the class, which could only be answered by the use of a particular skill, and her pupils learned about the Portuguese on the Zambezi by exercising the skills specified in the lesson objectives.

Why use a textbook to teach history?

As a resource, the average history textbook is very similar to the 'reference book', and in fact most history textbooks are written according to the same plan as a secondary reference of any kind: a continuous explicatory narrative covering a given period or set of topics. A textbook in history therefore differs considerably from a textbook in geography or mathematics. In the latter the pupil is taken through a graded series of exercises by which both the skills and the knowledge required by the discipline are learned. Although history texts may contain useful charts, illustrations, maps, and some questions to be answered, they are not organized according to to any sequential acquisition of skill. The sequence is wholly in the story or narrative. What 'grades' history textbooks is the language used to explain topics and the simplicity of treatment offered. But the lack of any skill sequence in history textbooks does not mean that there are no skills to be acquired in history. It means simply that the teacher has to organize the learning of skills because the textbook writers have not done it for him.

Nowadays, perhaps because they realize that the standard text is not really a textbook at all, publishers are beginning to produce reference books for schools, as well as what is referred to as 'stimulus' material: archival packs, workcards, etc. The greater the variety of material produced for the teacher, the easier it is to organize lessons according to the skill requirements of the pupils as well as their knowledge requirements. But the bulk of books published create a bank of information in an easily accessible form without which history teaching would be even more difficult than it is.

While history is gathered in the first instance from primary evidence, all historians need ready access to the results of other people's research. In the academic world monographs, published theses, and articles in learned journals serve this purpose. In schools students need specially selected written material, suitable in style and format for an adolescent to use in a classroom or library. In most areas of historical inquiry there is no lack of history text-books. The teacher is often at a loss to choose one from the many offered to him. But it is important that the book, once chosen, is not left to gather dust in lockers or desks. Textbooks are a resource for learning and, considering the expense involved in their purchase, pupils should be encouraged and taught how to use them.

Varieties of learning through textbooks

'In no other subject is there so much teaching and so little learning.' This statement is taken from a well-known text on history teaching, and it refers to the habit of those teachers who spend most of their time lecturing and little of it making the pupils do something from which they will learn. Some teachers simply ignore textbooks altogether. They regard them as a supplement to teaching, and do not feel that their particular method of teaching needs that sort of supplementation, although it is there if the pupils want to use it—if they know how to use it. Other teachers go to the opposite extreme. The textbook becomes the 'Bible'. Its contents must be known for examinations. All teaching activities are related to the study of this one resource: reading in class, making summaries for homework and undergoing factual tests based on the information it contains. This practice can be particularly harmful if only one textbook is used, since no history writing is entirely free from bias, and uncritical subjection to the same bias for long periods might dull the pupils' perceptiveness to that particular type of distortion.

For intelligent classroom use a textbook or any reference book should be treated critically. One text should be compared with other texts. Statements should be questioned. Bias should be identified. This is not always easy. The national or cultural bias of a foreign society is always more easy to spot than the beam in one's own eye. And a great deal of bias is cultural rather than 'patriotic', deriving, as one historian has put it, from an author 'weaving schoolmasterly injunctions into texts that purport to be about the historical past'. As this is something that every teacher (at every level) can be tempted to do, it may not be readily recognizable in a written text. Teachers should be critical of the texts they put before their pupils, and that requires of course that they do not rely on one authority. The teacher should be able to measure the textbook against his own personal resource library, and measure its contents against standards established by others.

Using a textbook properly is a skill which needs to be taught. Pupils are often left to themselves to find out what use can be made of the books which have been issued or which they have been required to buy. In particular, pupils need to be assisted in:

a) *Reference skills*   These include finding information, using indexes, sub-headings, etc.
b) *Comprehension skills*   These may concern the written text (the meanings of words and phrases, the connections between ideas) or charts, maps, diagrams, etc. Translation from one medium (e.g. a written paragraph) to another (a time-line) is a basic way of exercising pupils in simple comprehension of a passage.
c) *Analytical and critical skills*   Pupils need to be taught to read with a question in the backs of their minds: to look for the explanation to a particular problem. This habit will teach them not only to read with intelligence, but mentally to categorize their reading and treat what they read critically and methodically.

d) *Imaginative skills* Textbooks and other resources provide factual material for imaginative exercises. A well-written book can encourage a pupil to enter imaginatively into a period or episode. The teacher can use the book to give the information and set the historical parameters to an exercise in imaginative writing.

e) *Note-making skills* This is such an important skill both for history learning and for general educational development that a separate model has been devoted to it in this book. It does, however, require in some way a synthesis of the other skills involved in the intelligent study of texts.

Teacher's guide

What to avoid
In practice teachers should avoid too much reading aloud of a textbook. 'Reading round the class' is a barren activity, and the teacher's own reading is best limited to those passages where intelligent enunciation will make difficult prose intelligible. The use of the textbook should be structured around exercises which will ensure that the reading contributes to learning. For instance, instead of asking pupils to read five pages of a book for their homework, the teacher can pose a problem and ask pupils to solve it by means of their homework reading. Secondly, teachers should avoid relying too much on one book. If there is only one text available for the class, then comparison with reference books in the school library, or an occasional cyclostyled extract from a different source will teach pupils that texts are to be considered critically.

Possible exercises
Exercises should derive from the skill requirements of a particular class and the 'skill possibilities' of a particular topic. Some of the more obvious examples which can be structured on a secondary text are listed below:

Comprehension questions These are set on selected pages of the textbook. At any level of learning, the comprehension expectation of the teacher (or lecturer) almost always exceeds the performance of the students. Such exercises are therefore as good for the teacher as they are for the pupils.

Imaginative questions Information given in rather unimaginative ways in a textbook can be used to create a vivid picture or incident. People who are natural *aficionados* of history tend to do this automatically: to 'live' the passage as they read it. Average pupils can be taught to do it in easy exercises.

Compilation of data relevant to a problem Lists of data in a particular category can be extracted from a diffuse text. This will teach more than simple categorization: it will help pupils to test whether the text provides the sort of evidence upon which generalizations can be made.

Making diagrams, charts, etc. Information given in writing can be turned into a graphic or diagrammatic form as a simple exercise in translation.

Reference tasks A basic skill in historical (or any other) inquiry is the use of both the indicators given within books (indexes, etc.) and the indicators given about books (categorized lists, etc.).

Selecting a textbook
No teacher is going to find a history textbook which will do all his work for him. As has been suggested above, the majority of them simply tell the story. Structured exercises tend to be published separately as 'stimulus material'. The teacher will therefore have to select a book which will be in keeping with his own approach to teaching a topic or period, bearing in mind the availability of other resources both for himself and his pupils. If he wants a book mainly as a data bank for the curriculum of the year, then he will have a wide choice of traditional textbooks, and he ought to select after comparing various publishers' offerings and taking into account the following:

Coverage Textbooks are rarely written for a single syllabus, and it is usually difficult to find a book that will cover adequately all the topics any individual teacher might want to teach. Maximum coverage will be an important criterion.

Language   This includes a suitable vocabulary range and also a suitable style. History books tend to be written above the heads of those for whom they are intended. While this may have the effect of usefully 'stretching' the good student, a satisfactory textbook should be adapted to the needs of all the pupils who will use it. So a textbook at secondary level should rely strongly on concrete imagery rather than on abstractions or clichés. It should explain the variety of meanings for technical or specifically historical terms. It should be simple enough in style to be understood and be lively without being flippant. // — comic

Accuracy   It is surprising how often howlers appear in books from the most reputable of publishers. But accuracy does not simply mean the absence of errors. Textbooks should be balanced in approach, and should not present a misleading picture. Bias is bound to be there to some extent, but the teacher will try to identify that bias, and may even make use of it in historical explanation.

Arrangement   Nowadays most school books are suitably divided with chapters, headings, sub-headings, etc. to make reading simpler and reference quicker and easier in the classroom. The teacher must take care that a multiplicity of division does not disguise a lack of content coverage. Space is an expensive factor in books, and the teacher will make sure that it is well used in the book on which he is going to spend his own, his pupils', or the state's money.

Attractiveness   Again, publishers no longer issue the dull books of fifty years ago. But illustrations, maps, or diagrams should be devices of learning, not merely relief to the monotony of print.

Price   If the class is to have the opportunity to compare texts, or to compare a textbook with reference material, it is important that the whole budget should not be devoted to one item. Cheaper of course does not necessarily mean *better,* but cheaper can mean *more.*

Textbook study

Exercises

1 Take a page from any school history textbook. Assess the book, giving marks on a five-point scale for each of the items listed in the preceding section on 'Selecting a textbook'.
2 Spend ten minutes with a micro-teaching group studying one page of a textbook. By oral questioning make sure the pupils can understand the passage, place it in its historical context, and assess the information in it for accuracy or usefulness.
3 Teach a forty-minute lesson on one topic, using:
   a) a page of text, to be studied and understood;
   b) a map or diagram from the same book.

Further reading

Department of Education and Science, *Teaching History: Education Pamphlet No 23,* HMSO (London, 1952).
E.H. Dance, *History the betrayer, a study in bias,* Hutchinson (London, 1960).
J.W. Hunt, 'Textbooks and their uses', in W. H. Burston and C.W. Green, *Handbook for history teachers,* first edition, Methuen (London, 1962).
Incorporated Association of Assistant Masters in Secondary Schools, *The teaching of history,* Cambridge University Press (London, 1966).
R.E. Crookall, *Handbook for history teachers in Africa,* Evans Brothers (London, 1972).
William Lamont (ed.), *The realities of teaching history: beginnings,* Chatto & Windus (London, 1972).

5
Note-making

The teacher has just finished the first part of his lesson. For ten minutes he has been discussing with the class the strategic position of Iran in the post-war world, and its geographical place between Russia and British India as part of its political inheritance. This is a fourth-year class, studying a 'world history' syllabus with a standard textbook as the main resource. Having summarized, with the help of the pupils' suggestions, the perennial problems of the area, the teacher asks the class to open their texts at a certain page and read quietly for a few minutes four paragraphs on the post-war history of Iran. When they have done this he begins to ask some questions:

'The title of this sub-section in the textbook is "Persia", with "Iran" after it in brackets. Now this is not a very helpful or satisfactory title for the passage, which does not deal with the whole of Persian history. From what you have read in these four paragraphs can anyone suggest a better over-all title?'

Several alternatives are suggested: 'Russia, Britain, and Persia', 'Post-war Persia', 'Persia between the Great Powers', 'Persia and the problem of oil'. Finally the class agrees on 'Iran after the Second World War' (mainly because this is what the teacher himself obviously favours).

'Good, now look again at the first paragraph. Can anyone suggest a sub-heading as a title for that? Remember that we want to sum- marize in the title the main theme of the paragraph.' ('Persia after the war', 'Persia and the Communists', 'Persia up to 1946', are among various suggestions made.)

'Now listen. The whole passage is about post-war Iran, correct? Well, what is the most important aspect of the immediate post-war period that the author is trying to convey in this paragraph?'

'The fact that the Russians had a lot of influence there.'

Note-making

'Good, now that main idea should be summarized in your title. "Persia after the war" does not tell us anything about the content of the paragraph; it merely gives us a time-dimension. Try again.'

'Russian influence in Iran.' After several more attempts the class comes up with something the teacher feels is acceptable and they continue.

'There are three sentences in this passage. We want now to pick out the essential points, the points the author is trying to put across. Now look at the first sentence. Do you think it contributes in any way to the theme which we have expressed in the sub-heading, "Russian influence in Iran"? No. It is really a piece of introductory waffle. It makes the passage easier to read but it is not essential. Now who can list the four main activities of the Russians in Iran as given in the next few sentences?'

This part is more difficult. Everyone can list three: the Russian occupation of part of Iran, Russian encouragement of Communism and separatism, and Russia's leaving the occupied territory in 1946.

'Well, perhaps you are right. There were only three activities. But is there anything left out? There is one important word in the paragraph which has not been mentioned in the summary we have made so far. Can anyone spot it?'

'Yes sir, oil.'

'Indeed, oil. Now this was not an activity. How can we put it down, as what?'

'It was what they were really after, sir.'

'Correct, so that is how you can summarize it: Russians after Iranian oil.'

And having thus completed an agreed set of phrases summarizing the paragraph, the teacher writes them on the board and turns with the class to the next paragraph and the next sub-heading, and so on until the section is finished and a complete set of notes appears: a combined effort of pupils and the teacher. Teacher and pupils then begin examining the position taken by the author of the text.

Objectives

The teacher's lesson objectives can be seen from his lesson plan, which appears as Figure 6. You will note from the plan that there

Lesson plan: Fourth Year
Topic: Iran since Second World War.
Apparatus: Textbook
            Wall map of world
Objectives: 1. Students should summarize the main outline
              of post-war developments in Iran.
             2. Given the textbook passage, students should
              make notes with guidance.
             3. Students should detect the author's bias
              in the textbook.

Method: Teacher exposition on general historical
         background in the Middle East.
         Class note-making session, guided by teacher's
         questioning. Class discussion on the attitude
         of the author.

Content: Background: Iran the centre of ancient empire,
                     became Muslim. Feudal system
                     survived into twentieth century.
                     Nineteenth-century rivalry between
                     Britain and Russia, neither get
                     control of Iran. Modernization after
                     Frist World War superficial.
         Iran since Second World War: in textbook.
         Attitude of author: strongly in favour of Shah.
                          Note choice of words and
                          comparison with Chile.

Figure 6   Lesson plan: note-making

were three main activities: the expository introduction, the note-making session, and the critical examination of the author's standpoint. The first objective, summarizing the developments, was achieved by the first two activities. The main part of the lesson was devoted to guided note-making, which was the second objective. The third objective was to identify bias in the passage.

One of the main elements of the teacher's lesson which does not appear in the plan was his own set of notes, the model towards which he was guiding the class. This is given as Figure 7. In fact the notes which finally appeared on the board were not exactly the same as those in the model, but they were substantially the same. The model shows that the teacher had a definite type of note in mind for his class and that his intention was to train pupils not just to summarize paragraphs, but to write history notes in a particular way. We need not suppose that he would have rejected any other model. There is no single way of making notes to which all scholars subscribe. But he was right in that to develop any skill the teacher must use one definite method. Once the principles behind note-making have been mastered, and that will take some time, pupils can adapt the method to suit their own preferred way of working. But the aim is always an efficient summary, in the form of notes.

Why make notes?

The tyranny of notes has for long been recognized as one of the most deadly faults of much history teaching and examining. Copying notes from the board, taking them down on dictation, scanning reams of grubby cyclostyled sheets, learning notes off by heart for tests or examinations: all these things contribute to the terrible boredom and lifelessness which spoils history for so many pupils. Why then, in a book devoted to the promotion of interesting activities in history, should we insist on notes?

Well, partly to correct those faults of history teaching which we have listed above. Books on teaching have condemned the standard, boring practices for many, many years, and yet they still go on. Perhaps because teachers are not always offered an alternative to the practices condemned. And perhaps because, despite what people

Iran since Second World War: Notes

Russian influence:

- Russians occupied northern half of country
- encouraged Communist Party and separatist movements in Caucasus
- interested in Caucasian oil
- withdrew in 1946 under United Nations pressure.

Moussadek Grovemment 1951-3:

- replaced a series of weak govemments in 1951
- nationalized Anglo-Iranian Oil Company
- this produced marketing difficulties and a financial crisis
- Moussadek deposed in 1953

Shah's govemment, 1953 to present:

- marketing agreement reached with Anglo-Iranian Oil (B.P.)
- wealth from oil used to raise standard of living
- improvements in agriculture, industry, communications, medical services
- land reforms divided up estates and broke power of landlord class
- land given to peasants and new class of smallholders emerged

Foreign affairs:

- Iran is member of CENTO (military alliance dominated by U.S.A.)
- moving towards non-alignment, Iran is challenging Egypt's leadership of Arab world.

Figure 7   Model notes

say, teachers remain convinced that notes are useful.

In this they may not be completely wrong. It is probably true that many teachers who argue in this way are concerned with the examination potential of good notes. The better the notes, the clearer, the more complete, the more concise they are, the easier will be the tiresome chore of revision upon which so much is supposed (often mistakenly) to depend. Well, history does not exist solely for the purpose of enabling people to pass exams, although many teachers may feel that that is what *they* exist for. And while notes are certainly easier to remember than pages of text, any well written examination in history demands more than just memory skills. But if a pupil has composed his notes himself, then whether they are of much value for revision or not, he will have gained something useful from them.

Writing notes from a text requires several quite complicated skills. The pupil has first to select his material, he then has to assemble it in a logical fashion; he has to compress many words into few, and express the main ideas concisely, without making them so cryptic that in six months' time he cannot understand what he has written. All these skills are valuable learning exercises. It is axiomatic that the pupil learns best if he is able to do something with the knowledge he is acquiring. Making notes out of it is one thing he can do. The act of making notes deepens his comprehension of the text he is studying or forces him to make testing comparisons if he is using more than one text. Making notes should take pupils into the heart of written matter, and although some teachers may complain that the heart is likely to be destroyed in the note-making attempts of their charges, the answer lies not in preventing pupils from getting at the heart, but in training them to recognize it, and respect it when they see it.

If history is not solely for the purpose of passing examinations it should have some educational relevance to adult life, for which secondary schooling is supposed to be a preparation. The value of the discipline of history in the mental development of adolescents has been mentioned in the introduction. But history as a discipline also involves intellectual skills which can be used in many walks of adult life, no matter where they are learnt. Most adults who have been subjected to secondary schooling have to do some paper work at least occasionally during their lives. They need to be able to categorize and classify what they read, to summarize reports, or to make written reports out of minutes taken in summary form. They need to be able to extract the salient points of an argument and record them in such a way that they can recall them when necessary. In an office, in administration, in higher education or training, note-making skills are essential. And although secondary school history is not intended solely to provide job-seekers with commercial or administrative skills, its contribution to general intellectual development should not be ignored.

Learning to make notes

There are several distinct types of note commonly used in history studies. Note-taking from lectures, which is common in universities or training colleges, is not a normal activity in secondary schools. Secondary school pupils might be asked to make notes from a written text:

a) to provide a summary of what an author has said;
b) to summarize those statements made by the author which are relevant to a specific theme.

Notes made for revision or for comprehension purposes fall into category (a), as do the notes made in the lesson quoted above. Category (b) notes are required if a pupil is preparing an essay. He takes from the author only what is relevant to the essay topic and arranges the notes in an order which suits that topic rather than in the order established by the author. In both types of note a logical sequence with headings and sub-headings is useful, for both types need to be used some time after they have been written and should be clear, concise, and complete.

In order to establish how a teacher should go about teaching note-making it is important to determine what distinct skills the activity requires. First, it certainly demands comprehension. Any activity that contributes towards understanding also contributes eventually towards mastery in note-making. Secondly, it requires the skill of categorizing. This concept includes the ability to distinguish between principles and specific examples, or between matter which is more or less relevant to the main topic or argument.

Finally, it requires the skills of summarizing and organizing material in a logical manner.

In the junior forms of a secondary school there is often little need for formal note-making. In countries where a large proportion of the secondary population leaves school after the junior forms it is obviously useful to develop note-making skills rather earlier, but it is usually best to leave exercises in formal note-making as late as possible, until they are needed within the school curriculum, and to concentrate in the earlier years on activities that develop other skills related to note-making.

As a first stage, for example, pupils in the first year can be given short passages and asked to express the main ideas in them. They can be given comprehension exercises on short passages. They can be asked to write headings for paragraphs in the textbook. They can be given sets of assertions and asked to arrange them in order of importance or asked to distinguish statements which are general principles from those which are examples. They can be asked to categorize events according to relationships of cause and effect. One very common activity is a 'fill-the-blanks' exercise in which pupils copy an incomplete text and have to insert appropriate words or phrases in the spaces left by the teacher. While this exercise is often favoured because of its simplicity it needs to be used with caution, since it frequently calls for a mere parrot-like repetition of key phrases from the original text which may not have been fully understood.

Once pupils have mastered the basic contributory skills they can be instructed in note-making by being required to follow a set procedure, with guidelines in the early stages to make that procedure more comprehensible. The lesson described earlier in this chapter was a first step in this process. The teacher was following the procedure, asking his class questions which would elicit notes of the approved kind. The next stage is to get pupils to write notes themselves, again with the teacher's questions or comments. Gradually these guidelines can be reduced as pupils acquire the ability to ask questions of the material for themselves. When they can sit in front of a text and write commendable notes without any help at all they can be considered to have mastered the skill. At what stage in secondary schooling this ought to happen depends on many variables: the general educational organization of the area, the ages at which pupils pass through secondary schools, and their linguistic and other abilities.

Teacher's guide

What to avoid

Avoid dictating notes to the class. Dictation may have its place in language studies, but it can easily kill all interest in history. Avoid writing lengthy notes on the board for children to copy. Some copying from the board may be helpful, but to make it the usual or even the only way of getting pupils to write notes is quite wrong. Where textbooks are in short supply, avoid making pupils copy notes which are meant to act as a substitute for a book. If such material is necessary then the teacher should have it duplicated and distributed to the pupils. Notes are not meant to be a substitute for a text, but a means of mastering the contents of a text. Finally, avoid placing too much emphasis on 'fill-the-blanks' exercises. At a very early stage they may have their uses, but if pupils do not quickly go beyond that stage of note-making then there is probably something wrong with the teaching method.

Here are some examples of the kind of exercises suggested above, which first develop contributory skills and then train in note-making itself:

Comprehension exercise

Trade at Ingombe Ilede

Perhaps the trade worked in this way. The people at Ingombe Ilede would sell salt to the villages north and south of the river. In exchange they would receive copper from the north and gold from the south. They might also have received slaves. The copper, gold and slaves were collected at Ingombe Ilede with local ivory. The traders from the coast came up the river with beads, shells, cloth and perhaps hoes and other tools. They exchanged these at the market and took away the copper, gold, slaves and ivory to the coast. Now the people of Ingombe Ilede would have beads, shells and cloth to sell to the surrounding peoples. The buying and selling could start all over again.
[*From:* S. Johnston, *Early Man in Zambia,* Oxford University Press (East Africa, 1971).]

Note-making

a) Make a list of four different groups of people who were trading.
b) Beside each item on your list put the goods that they sold.
c) Then put in brackets the goods that they bought.
d) Now underline on your list the goods they sold which they had not produced themselves.

Summarizing exercise

Life in Cape Colony

By the end of the eighteenth century there were fifteen thousand white people at the Cape. They were ruled by the Dutch East India Company (the firm which owned the trading ships) and they had a Governor of the Colony. Cape Town was the only real town, and here the traders lived. Their houses had thatched roofs and white walls, and inside they were well furnished with materials sent from Holland. In the Governor's house there were dishes and cups of silver, and the Dutch built a Christian church which had silver and gold ornaments. Every church in the Colony contained a Bible; the Dutch did not have many other books and they all knew the Bible thoroughly.

Outside Cape Town the people lived in farmhouses which they built themselves, or else moved from place to place with their cattle as the grazing became poor. The soil in the Colony was never very good for agriculture. Each farm was far away from the next, and those who settled in the north of the Colony were hundreds of miles from Cape Town. They had a very hard life, which made them tough and brave. They were quite cut off from their own country, and for years on end they didn't know what was happening in the rest of the world. Their only visitors were traders from Cape Town who brought goods for them to buy in exchange for cattle and sheep, which the traders then took on foot back to Cape Town market.

[*From:* Margaret Sharman, *Africa through the ages,* Evans Brothers (London, 1964).]

a) What is the first paragraph about?
b) What is the second paragraph about?
c) Give each paragraph a sub-heading.

Categorizing exercise

a) Make a list of all the pre-colonial African kingdoms you have learned about.
b) Divide the kingdoms into three groups:

   (i) those in West Africa;
   (ii) those in East and Central Africa;
   (iii) those in Southern Africa.
c) From your original list make two more groups:
   (i) those which developed because of trade;
   (ii) those which developed because of other reasons.
d) From your original list make three more groups:
   (i) those which disappeared before European colonization;
   (ii) those which were destroyed by European colonization;
   (iii) those which survived colonization but became weaker.

Exercise on distinguishing general principles from specifics

From the following sentences pick out those which are general
statements and match them with those which are examples:
a) In East Africa Swahili traders sometimes became kings and
   established their own kingdoms based on the ivory and slave
   trade.
b) Mirambo, an unimportant chief of the Nyamwezi, was able to
   build a big empire through trading.
c) Migrations from the south helped to destroy Central African
   states which were already weakened.
d) The development of the East African caravan trade in the
   nineteenth century had important effects on African societies.
e) At first the Portuguese traded with Mwenemutapa, but in the
   end they gained control of the trade for themselves and his big
   trading empire gradually disappeared.
f) The Chewa kingdom of Undi was too weak to resist the Ngoni
   of Zwangendaba and broke up when he invaded.
g) The Swahili Tippu Tip formed a large kingdom west of Lake
   Tanganyika.
h) Many African kingdoms were destroyed by European
   incursion.

Note-making exercise with guidelines

The Five Year Plan and Collectivization

By 1926 Russian industry and agriculture had reached their pre-war
rate of production. Any further economic progress with existing
plant would be low, and if the standard of living was to be raised
and Russia was to be stronger economically it was clear that new
plant and the expansion and modernization of industry and
agriculture were necessary. Further, if Russia was to be strong
militarily, the country would have to make economic progress. 'We
are fifty or a hundred years behind the advanced countries', said

Stalin in 1931. 'We must make good this lag in ten years. Either we do this or they crush us.'

Stalin therefore aimed at very rapid industrialization, and he intended to achieve this with the help of agriculture. He reasoned that in order to buy the necessary foreign machinery agricultural exports would have to be increased. This would be done by reorganizing the 25 million peasant households so that very large farms were formed. These would help mechanization and would help make grain collection easier, and would reduce the amount of labour needed so that excess labour would move to the towns. These new farms would therefore be more efficient and would therefore produce more goods more cheaply. Cheaper agricultural produce would mean firstly that urban wages could be reduced so that manufacturing costs would go down, and secondly, that exports would increase so that there could be more imports of capital goods. Stalin also believed that this revolution in the economy would be good in two other ways: it would be sound ideologically in that it implied much greater state control and fewer class divisions in society, and secondly, it would require force to carry it through and therefore the strong leadership which Stalin could provide was essential.

The revolution in farming began in 1928 and reached its height in 1930. Large collective farms were formed by amalgamating groups of about twenty small farms. Land, except for small private plots, was taken from private ownership, and the peasants who worked the collective farm owned it in common. Wages were paid according to the time spent working on the collective farm. Most of the produce, which was mainly grain, had to be sold to the state at low prices.

Even the poorer peasants did not like collectivization, but the richer peasants, who were known as kulaks, violently opposed the loss of their land. Stalin's answer was to 'liquidate the kulaks as a class'. Red Army units rounded up the kulaks and killed them or deported them to labour camps. The kulaks in retaliation killed their cattle, destroyed their machinery and burned their crops. 'Collectivization degenerated into a military operation, a cruel, civil war. Rebellious villages were surrounded by machine guns and forced to surrender. Great numbers of kulaks were deported to remote unpopulated lands in Siberia. Their houses, barns and farm implements were turned over to the collective farms.'

Between 1930 and 1934 Stalin slowed down the process of collectivization, but nevertheless by 1937 99 per cent of farmland was collective. The result was, on the whole, disastrous. The immediate chaos led to poor harvests and a famine in which over 10 million people died (and during which Russia continued to export grain). The best farmers had been liquidated, the peasants were depressed and resentful, the numbers of livestock were halved, the younger and more energetic peasants had left for the towns, and, moreover, the new collective farms proved less productive than those they had replaced.

Meanwhile industrialization was proceeding apace. The first Five Year Plan was started in 1928 and was declared complete after four years. The emphasis was on heavy industry—coal, iron, steel, oil, electricity, machine-building. For economic and strategic reasons, the new industries were mainly sited away from the western frontiers: for example, a new iron and steel industry was started in the Urals. The second Five Year Plan (1932-7) again concentrated on heavy industry. There was more technical assistance from abroad and, although the plan was mainly underfulfilled and the quality of goods remained poor, there was still a great increase in production. The third Five Year Plan (1937-42) put more emphasis on consumer goods, but the dangerous foreign situation soon led to a switch to arms production.

The State Planning Commission was responsible for all the plans. It collected statistics and decided on targets for each industry and each individual firm within an industry. Since a failure to reach a target could lead to imprisonment, figures for production were often exaggerated by managers. In general, too, the plans were too inflexible and failed to make the best use of resources: oil production was slowed down in favour of coal; too many canals were built rather than roads and railways. And the cost in human suffering was great (compare the English industrial revolution in the nineteenth century); the standard of living fell continually.

Nevertheless industrial production made huge strides forward. Russia was transformed from an agrarian into an industrial country. Also, there is evidence that many workers responded to the propaganda for increased production. Distinctions such as 'Hero of Socialist Labour' were soon augmented by wages based on piece rates and other financial inducements which reversed the trend towards equality of incomes.

[*From:* R.D. Cornwell, *World history in the twentieth century,* Longmans (1969).]

Make notes on the Five Year Plans and collectivization following these guidelines:
a) Read the whole passage. Write down a general summary in two sentences.
b) Read the first paragraph. What is it about? Answer in one sentence. Give the paragraph a sub-heading. Under your sub-heading write notes on the following: Give three reasons why Stalin wanted to introduce a programme of rapid industrialization.

Note-making

c) Read the second paragraph. What is it about? Give it a sub-heading. Then write notes by answering these questions:
   (i) Why did Stalin want to increase agricultural production?
   (ii) Why did Stalin want to introduce collective farms?
d) Read the third paragraph. What is it all about? Give it a sub-heading. Then write three notes describing how collective farms were created.
e) Read the fourth paragraph. What is it all about? Give it a sub-heading. Under your sub-heading write notes on the results of collectivization.
f) Read the fifth paragraph. What is it all about? Give it a sub-heading. Then write notes answering these questions:
   (i) What was the main aim of the first Five Year Plan?
   (ii) Where were most of the industries built?
   (iii) Describe the second Five Year Plan and say what happened to it.
   (iv) Describe the third Five Year Plan and say what happened to it.
g) Read the last paragraph. What is it about? Give it a sub-heading. Then answer the questions:
   (i) Which body did the planning?
   (ii) What were its methods?
h) Write a summary of the whole passage by answering the following question: What were the achievements of Russia in this period and what was the cost in human terms? Compare this summary with the one you made above in (a).

Exercises

1 Select a passage of about two hundred words from a textbook used in junior secondary forms and prepare:
   a) a set of comprehension questions on the passage;
   b) a set of questions on summarizing;
   c) a set of questions on categorizing.
2 Select a passage of not more than a page and a half from a senior secondary textbook and prepare:
   a) a set of notes;
   b) a set of guidelines for note-making as given above.
3 With micro-teaching groups, read a short passage of about two hundred lines from any historical text and try, by your questioning, to get the pupils to summarize the argument in a short set of notes.

4   Conduct a lesson on note-making with a class which has not been instructed in this skill before. Try to assess the ability of the pupils in answering the questions posed by the teacher and asking questions of the text for themselves. Work out how many lessons and how many assignment exercises you think this class will need before it will be able to make notes unaided.

Further reading

R.E. Crookall, *Handbook for history teachers in Africa,* second edition, Evans Brothers (London, 1972).

W.H. Burston, 'The history teacher and the G.C.E.' in W.H. Burston and C.W. Green, *Handbook for history teachers,* first edition, Methuen (London, 1962).

Harry McNicol, *History, heritage and environment*, Faber (London, 1946).

6
Map study

The teacher has been giving a series of lessons on the growth of international conflict in the Middle East from the First World War period up to the outbreak of the Yom Kippur War of 1973. With the help of a textbook and a wall map she has led the class through the history of Jewish and Arab Nationalism to the partition war of 1948-9. Now, before dealing with the clashes of 1956 and 1967, she is taking a closer look at the small area of land about which there has been so much violent controversy. For this purpose she has prepared and cyclostyled a sketch-map (Figure 8) which shows the principal physical features of the area and the post-1949 political boundaries. There are no names on the map but the teacher has printed letters near the places of political significance.

At the beginning of this lesson she revises quickly by asking her pupils to identify the places which should be familiar to them.

'What is that piece of land marked B?'

'The Gaza Strip.'

'And what do you know about it which makes it important in the relations between the new Isael and other states?'

'Refugees . . . . The strip contained settlements of Arab refugees from Palestine after the partition war.'

'And what about the area marked F? What is that?'

'That must be the West Bank.'

When the revision is completed, the teacher invites her pupils to look more closely at certain features on the sketch-map.

'Look at the shape of the state of Israel, as it was after the end of the war in 1949. You see it is in several sections: a coastal strip, and an inland area near a lake—what lake is that by the way?'

'The Sea of Galilee.'

'Yes, but nowadays it is usually known by another name. Does

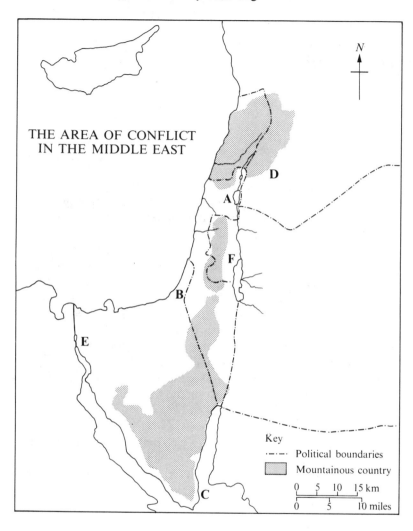

Figure 8   Map of the Middle East

anybody know it? Well, you ought to know about it if only to realize
what people are talking about when they mention Lake Tiberias.
The third area is the southern triangle reaching down to the Gulf of
Aqaba. Now this area was larger than that recommended by the
partitioning authorities. This was land held by Israel after winning
a war, so we can assume that it was largely what the Israelis wanted.
But why did they want those three areas in particular? Let us start
with the coastal strip: what advantage had the control of that strip
for Israel?'

'The coast was fertile.'

'Trade with the west went on from coastal ports.'

'Tel Aviv on the coast had become the main Jewish city.'

'Yes, there seem to be plenty of worthwhile reasons for wanting
to control the Mediterranean coast. But what now about the inland
area, joined by a narrow belt to the coast. The Israelis had enlarged that belt by means of war, but why did they need to? What
was the value of the land in the interior?'

'Weren't there kibbutzes in that area?'

'Well, if there were, why were they there and not elsewhere?
Why not for instance further south on the edge of that other lake?'

This question causes some difficulty. And it is only after some
prompting that the class remembers the infertility of the Dead Sea
area in comparison with the coast of Lake Tiberias. Similar
questioning leads the class to deduce the strategic reasons for an
opening through desert land to the Gulf of Aqaba and the Indian
Ocean.

'Now there is one small area which we have not yet looked at.
Look on your maps at the central portion of the eastern frontier of
Israel. You notice how the border runs in a more-or-less straight
line down the edge of the mountains, except at one point where there
is an indentation. There Israel took over a block of hill country.
Then the frontier moves back to the edge of the hills and runs south.
Now why is there that indentation? What were the Israelis
interested in there?'

Somebody quickly points out that Jerusalem is situated near the
indentation and the teacher uses the opportunity to discuss with the
class the relationship between economic, strategic, religious, and
political motivation in the general conflict. Then the attention of
the class is directed to the strategic problems which led to the

fighting of 1956. As a homework assignment the pupils are told to trace on their maps the lines of battle in the 1956 war, taking the information from a brief paragraph in their textbooks.

Objectives

For the lesson described above, the teacher had three distinct objectives. With a sketch-map of the area of the Arab-Israeli conflict, the pupils should firstly, identify the places of strategic importance to Israel, secondly, work out and understand the motives for controlling the areas held by Israel after 1949, thirdly, comprehend the economic and strategic considerations which led to the invasion of Sinai in 1956.

Since this lesson was conducted orally by the teacher, just how much each pupil was doing in order to answer the questions posed and thus fulfil the lesson objectives could only be guessed. Hands went up, and the owners of those hands had presumably put their minds to the problems posed and were ready to offer solutions. But the others, whose hands did not appear, may have been struggling manfully if less successfully to find an answer, or may simply have been day-dreaming. The teacher could of course see that everyone was paying attention to the map which had been distributed, but she could not ensure that all her pupils were concentrating on her questions.

Not all classroom teaching can be individually oriented or conveniently organized in groups. Participation in joint efforts has sometimes to be invited rather than demanded. And the orientation of this lesson, with its reliance on a sketch-map, probably demanded the sort of teacher control which can only be ensured in a plenary session. The map gave a focus to the lesson and it gave an opportunity for the pupils to relate politics to locality and to seek for the influence of environment upon strategy. It was therefore a resource as well as an aid to history learning.

Why use maps in history teaching?

There are two basic ways in which maps can be used during a history lesson:

1   As an illustration or visual aid, which will help pupils to under-
    stand particular topics or episodes. If a teacher does not make
    use of maps or atlases it is because he presumes that the pupils
    are carrying mental atlases in their heads. Most pupils know
    enough of their local geography to be able to form mental
    pictures of their own native country and relate national history
    to geographic areas and conditions. But for international history,
    maps should be provided to show the proximity of certain areas
    and the political and geographic relationships between them. A
    map of the world is an obvious necessity in a properly equipped
    history room, and wall maps of greater detail are frequently
    used by teachers to illustrate particular lessons.

2   As a resource from which pupils can themselves learn history.
    Such learning may relate to specifically historical events—battles,
    migrations, trade routes, etc.—which can be found symbolized
    on historical maps or atlases. Or the learning may be more
    concerned with the interaction of geography and history, the
    relationship between the environment and the activities of people
    who have controlled or sought control of it. Ever since the study
    of economic motivation became a legitimate part of academic
    history, geography has been of paramount importance in
    constructing a satisfactory historical explanation.

If pupils are to understand the history they are being taught they
need to be able to read and use maps. In order to discover evidence
for causality and motivation, and learn to investigate as well as to
observe, pupils must be taught how to ask historical questions of
maps. They must learn how to match geographical factors with
historical events and how to include the environment and ecology
in their historical hypotheses. But to achieve this attitude to maps,
they need to be instructed and exercised in the use of geographical
resources for historical purposes. They need to use maps with their
teacher, as was done in the class described above, and to use them
individually in working out historical explanations.

Varieties of learning through maps
The types of lesson which can be taught using maps as a main resource
can be classified conveniently according to the kinds of map
provided and used by the teacher:

Historical maps   These are maps specially prepared and published with historical as well as geographical information. They require careful attention to the keys provided. They can be used to illustrate a narrative and the best textbooks (like the best teachers) will make good use of them. But they can also be used as a source of information. In other words, an historical map can be used like a textbook as an account of a given episode. And just as a written text can be translated into diagrammatic form, so the information given on an historical map can be turned by pupils into a written narrative. Such an exercise if done by a teacher could provide a demonstration of the way to read a story from a map. If it were done by pupils it would be a formative exercise in comprehension and a means of establishing how much use a particular class can make of diagram and symbol in historical reading.

Standard geography maps   The average school atlas contains a variety of types of map, some concentrating on physical, others on economic, and others (in that they show national boundaries) on political information. It is a strange but frequent phenomenon that many history teachers who complain of the lack of map material for their classes often neglect the standard resources of the school geography department. School atlases of course do not give specific historical information, but they can be used to train pupils in exploring the relationship between communities and the areas they inhabit, in looking for possible geographical aspects to historical events or in hypothesizing on the economic, strategic, or other advantages in the control or exploitation of a particular area of land or sea. The dynamic of history can also be seen in the changing value of land areas as exploiters move on or technologies advance, while the adverse effects of over-exploitation can be studied from the information given in standard atlases regarding rainfall, temperature, population, etc.

Maps prepared for class exercises   Maps can be prepared by teachers with a particular historical problem or exercise in mind. Such maps will contain whatever information the teacher wishes to include, and there may be as much pedagogical value in what has been left off the map (such as the place names in Figure 8) as in what has been put in. Most teachers probably prefer to prepare

Map study

their own maps if time permits, but it is certainly not possible for a teacher with more than a very light teaching load to produce and cyclostyle a sketch-map for every topic that requires one. Some publishers help teachers by the issue of 'sketch-map histories'. While the worst of these seem to be little more than badly drawn historical atlases, the better ones cover the main lines of chosen topics and even include exercises relating to historical material both symbolized on and omitted from the sketch.

Wall maps   If a map is to be used mainly as a visual aid, then a wall map which can be seen by the whole class is often perfectly sufficient. These may be published maps or may be specially drawn by the teacher. For national histories or the main lines of European or North American history there are plenty of useful published maps. The more recently researched topics of Asian or African history have not yet found their way into commercially produced wall maps and the teacher will often have to make his own. Such maps cannot conveniently be used for pupil exercises. Concentration on cartographic detail calls for individual maps, and wall maps, to be visible, should contain very few items.

Chalkboard maps   Many teachers use the board to draw quick maps during their exposition, as they might print new names or write the outline of their argument. Such maps, if drawn during class time, can only be rudimentary, and normally suppose that the pupils have access to a 'real' map, of which the chalkboard sketch is but a reminder. But it is often easier to pose an historical problem with a drawing on the board rather than by use of a commercial map which may have not enough or may even have too much information on it.

Teacher's guide

The choice of a map
A published wall map is normally chosen with the objectives of a lesson or series of lessons in mind. An important criterion in selecting a particular map is therefore its relevance to the lessons it is meant to serve. Since it will be used as a visual aid, it must be easy

to read from the back of a class. It needs therefore to be uncluttered, and must show enough information but not too much, with clear lines and print. Wall maps made by the teacher should also conform to these principles. Lettering needs to be at least two centimetres high to be clearly visible from the back of an average-sized classroom. Lines should be thick, made by felt markers or crayons rather than pens or pencils. And there should be a clear distinction, by means of variation in colouring or lettering style or size, between the more important information, which should stand out clearly, and the less important. Unless a teacher is especially gifted a map made with lettering stencils produces a much neater and clearer impression than one with freehand lettering. The acid test of a wall map is whether a child, viewing it from the back of a classroom, finds it an aid to understanding or is merely further confused by it.

Small maps in textbooks, atlases, etc., may be used if they are relevant. The main problem with some published historical atlases is that the maps often try to include too much material, and contain information which covers a long period. This is unhelpful to the pupil who is trying to understand the events which happened over a much shorter period. Published atlases should be scrutinized for accuracy as well as clarity and relevance. When teachers make their own small maps they should also take care to make them accurate, but they should still follow the conventions of normal cartography. A map should have a line around the edge, so that rivers do not trail off into space, and any physical feature should be shown in full. A range of mountains, for example, should be given its full extent within the boundaries of the map, not just shown at the place where it has historical significance. Scale and direction should be marked, even if the finished article is simply a sketch.

Maps drawn on the chalkboard during a lesson probably do not conform to these conventions, primarily because strictly speaking they are not maps at all but diagrams. If a teacher thinks of a chalkboard sketch as a geographic diagram of an historical problem, rather than as a conventional map, he will be less inhibited in his attempts to clarify difficult issues despite limited draughtsmanship. Figure 9 gives two examples of attempts made on a board to show the boundary problems of central Europe between the world wars. One is a rough attempt at ordinary map making. The other, laughable perhaps as a map, is a diagrammatic representation of

Map study

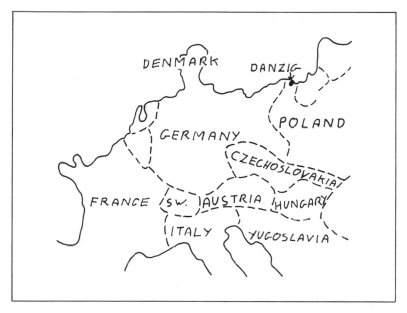

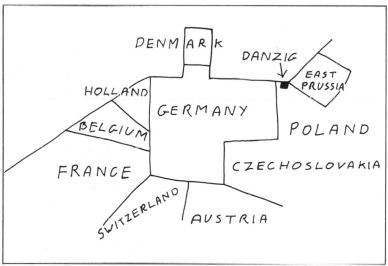

Figure 9   Two chalkboard maps

the geographic situation. Beautifully wrought maps in a variety
of colours are sometimes seen on chalkboards, obviously indicating
that a vast amount of time and care has been spent by a teacher in
preparing an attractive visual aid. It is a pity that it will soon have
to be rubbed off to make place for something less attractive! If a
map needs to be made with care and variety, it should really be
drawn on cartridge paper or similar material so that it can be
preserved, and used again.

Types of map exercises

Obtaining information from a map   Pupils need help and guidance
from teachers if they are to obtain historical information from
historical maps, school atlases or specially prepared maps. The
questions by which a teacher leads children to make the right sort
of inquiry of maps should follow the kind of sequence suggested
already for other forms of historical investigation. There should first
be general orientation questions which exercise simple map comprehension: What does the map show? On what scale? At what
period? Then specific data can be found from the map: Where did
the 1914 advance of the German armies reach closest to Paris?
The historical significance of those data should then be sought, and
hypotheses formed, drawing substance from the information given
on the map. How did the German advance differ from the original
plans made by Schlieffen and his successors? What tactical advantage
would there have been in an advance on Paris from the south as
Schlieffen suggested? This sort of sequence can be followed several
times in the study of a single map, as the teacher guides the pupils
in pursuit of different sets of information. But the success of
children in translating the information symbolized on the map and
forming a synthesis of the story it tells will depend, as ever, on the
teacher's skill at asking the right sort of questions.

Putting information on to maps   To put information on maps is
another very useful exercise in translation. Children can make use
of their historical knowledge, their understanding of cartographic
symbols, and their familiarity with a particular geographic area to
make an historical map for themselves. With this sort of activity it

should always be remembered that the primary purpose is historical rather than cartographic. Some children are made to spend tedious hours drawing map outlines freehand because their teacher believes it is 'cheating' to trace them. For history students the historical information and its meaning is important. Outline maps can be produced by mapograph or other techniques and distributed by the teacher so that pupils are concerned only with the completion of the historical picture. This may obviate one ever-present danger in history map exercises: that the history teacher presumes a higher standard of geographical skill of his class than the geography teacher expects for that level. Which brings us to another problem: How can the history teacher deal with pupils who seem unable to read maps?

Guided map reading   Maps are a form of communicating information which have their own language and symbol systems. Just as some pupils have difficulty in reading straightforward English, others have difficulties in reading maps. It is a skill which has to be learned, just as the skill of reading pictures must be learned. The skill is more advanced than that of picture reading however, because the symbols on maps are generally more abstract than representations on a picture.

It is not usually considered the function of a history teacher to train pupils in the language of maps. But the history teacher, besides finding out the level of geographic competence of his class and taking care not to demand more of them than the geography teacher would expect, invariably has to deal with some children who are below the class average. It is important to ensure before beginning any sort of map exercise that the pupils can read maps. This can be done by test questions: How far is it from X to Y on the map? Where is the highest land? How many areas of water are shown? If one or two pupils appear to be seriously below the level of most of the class they may need to be given further practice: an exercise in simply reading the historical map, for instance, rather than in interpreting it or working on it in other ways.

Organizing map study
As with other methods of learning history, map study can be organized in different ways. There are three basic alternatives:

a) *Class study*   Here the teacher presents the material orally and the pupils interact with the teacher while studying either their own maps or a map on the wall.

b) *Individual study*   Each pupil proceeds on his own, working on a map with the help of written questions.

c) *Group study*   One map may be used for each group, or each pupil may have a separate copy. The prepared questions in the map exercise should be answered by the group as a whole.

Exercises

1   Take and reproduce (or draw for yourself) an historical map relating to one specific topic. Write a series of questions aimed at getting a group of pupils to interpret and gain historical insight from the map. Your questions should follow the sort of sequence suggested above: comprehension, interpretation, and hypothesis.

2   During a ten-minute micro-teaching session, try to get your pupils to interpret a physical map in terms of an historical problem. Help them by oral questioning.

3   Teach a forty-minute practice lesson on a topic which allows for a map approach. Your objectives for the lesson should include the learning of specific information from a map and the development of skills of map-reading and interpretation.

Further reading

Incorporated Association of Assistant Masters in Secondary Schools, *The teaching of history,* third edition, Cambridge University Press (London, 1966).

E. West (ed.), *Improving the teaching of world history,* National Council for Social Studies (Washington, 1949).

7

Simulation and drama

The class has been divided into four groups, each assembled around a different set of tables. On the pin-board is a time-chart reminding the class of the constitutional developments in Central Africa from 1950 to 1960, and on the chalkboard the main lines of the 1959 'Benson Constitution' in Northern Rhodesia have been written. The groups are discussing intently but quietly, as it is important that they are not overheard. For this double period the classroom has become Lancaster House, London. The discussions in progress are the preliminaries of the Northern Rhodesian Constitutional Conference of 1961.

One of the four main groups represents the United Federal Party. Each member of the group has been given a policy sheet which reads as follows:

United Federal Party

You are the ruling party in the Central African Federation, but the Conference is for Northern Rhodesia only. You are represented here because of the United Federal Party members on the Northern Rhodesian Legislative Council.

Your main objective is to preserve (a) Federation and (b) white control of the Northern Rhodesian copper belt.

African majority rule has already been promised by the British Government to Nyasaland. This is a blow to your hopes of preventing African rule in Northern Rhodesia and therefore of preserving Federation, since it is certain that African political leaders will opt out of Federation if they are given power. You have no real hope of declaring successful unilateral independence from Britain for both the Rhodesias. Even if British troops did not intervene to prevent such independence, the seven thousand white troops in Southern Rhodesia could not manage to control eight million Africans in both territories, among whom are two thousand five hundred

African soldiers and four thousand African police. It might be worth threatening to declare unilateral independence for both Rhodesias as a bluff.

What constitutional change can you suggest at the Conference which might act as a sop to the Africans without actually giving them any power?

Another group represents the more moderate white Liberal Party.

The group is studying their policy, which reads as follows:

Liberal Party

You are a small inter-racial group, holding three seats on the legislative Council mainly because of African support. You are led and managed almost single-handed by Sir John Moffat.

The Liberal Party wants to see (a) inter-racial partnership, and (b) eventual African majority rule, attained without bloodshed or damage to inter-racial harmony. You hope that some programme which will lead to African majority rule in five years will be acceptable to both sides in the main dispute.

What constitutional programme would meet those objectives?

The two principal African parties have joined forces for this Conference and are discussing their platform as set out in the following paper:

African National Congress and
United National Independence Party

The two main nationalist parties are united in their approach to this Conference. There are some fundamental differences between them, for example, they have differing opinions on militancy, the possibilities of violent action, and the speed at which Africanization should take place in Northern Rhodesia.

The objectives you have agreed on are (a) to obtain a constitution which will bring about African majority rule either immediately or in the very near future, (b) to bring about the dissolution of the Central African Federation, (c) to prevent a violent confrontation with Southern Rhodesian troops and to persuade Britain to guarantee the defence of Northern Rhodesia if faced with a declaration of white independence.

What sort of constitutional change are you going to suggest to the British Government in order to bring about these objectives?

Lastly there is a British Government delegation, also preparing proposals according to the following guidelines:

Simulation and drama

British Government

Note there is a difference of opinion between Colonial Secretary Ian Macleod (responsible for Northern Rhodesia) who is on the liberal wing of the Conservative Party and who firmly believes in the sentiments of Macmillan's 'wind of change' speech, and Commonwealth Secretary Duncan Sandys (responsible for Federation) who has many interests in Southern Rhodesia and is certainly not on the liberal wing of his party.

The general policies of the British Government are (a) to preserve the Central African Federation if at all possible, (b) to change the constitution of Northern Rhodesia in a way that will satisfy African politicians for the time being without destroying Federation, (c) to avoid giving offence to the white politicians to the extent of encouraging them to declare unilateral independence. There is a firm policy that, whatever happens, British troops will not be sent to Central Africa. But the loss of prestige to Britain ensuing from unilateral independence must be avoided.

What constitutional proposals would you put forward to the other groups in furtherance of your policies?

After twenty minutes or so of discussion the members of the Conference, under the neutral chairmanship of their teacher, make their positions known. The UFP have nothing to say. They are not offering any proposals but will wait to hear the opinions of the others. The ANC/UNIP insist on immediate independence with a single assembly elected by universal suffrage without property or other qualifications or distinction of rolls. The Liberal Party however has gone back to the 1960 notion of separate rolls for two categories of voters. They suggest an 'A' roll based on property qualifications which will elect the same number of representatives as that elected by the 'B' roll which will consist of all resident adults not qualifying for inclusion in the 'A' roll. This should give African representatives immediate parity with the whites and open the way to African majority rule as and when Africans are elected from the 'A' roll. The British Government delegation has come up with even more ingenious proposals: the preservation of the Benson Constitution for the Northern Rhodesian Legislative Council, with some adjustments which will bring Africans nearer to parity, and a new form of Northern Rhodesian representation in the Federal parliament upon which delegation the Africans will have a clear majority.

The reading of the statements is followed by another ten minutes of group discussion at the end of which the UFP declares all the proposals unacceptable, the Liberal Party offers to compromise with the British Government suggestions and the ANC/UNIP insist on a single-roll manhood suffrage election for the Northern Rhodesian assembly and profess themselves uninterested in the make-up of representation at the Federal Parliament.

In the last quarter of an hour the teacher makes a comparison between the simulated Conference and the real thing. In 1961 the UFP boycotted the proceedings altogether once it became clear that Britain would not agree beforehand to reject any possibility of African majority rule. This meant that while the Conference was in progress, unofficial talks were being held between the UFP and the British Government. The African delegation was angered by these double meetings and called upon the British Government to stop negotiating outside the Conference. Eventually the meetings ended in deadlock without any conclusion being reached, just as happened in the classroom simulation.

Objectives

The objectives for this simulation activity had been written by the teacher as follows: 'Given materials on the policies and objectives of the delegations at the Lancaster House Conference and time to discuss the proposals in groups representing the delegations, the pupils should (a) gain an insight into the problems of preparing proposals for open discussion, (b) realize the limitations of open-forum discussion of sensitive political issues, and (c) understand the points of view of the different parties interested in the constitutional reform of Northern Rhodesia.'

At the end of the exercise the teacher realized that, although the simulation had gone with plenty of enthusiasm, there was no telling whether all the objectives of the lesson had been achieved. So at the beginning of the next history lesson a few days later a post-mortem was held. The pupils were asked what they thought that the simulation had taught them. All admitted that the main task given to the Conference was an impossibility. Given the disparity of views and interests, no delegation was likely to accept openly the suggestions of any other delegation. This made the whole exercise, as a political manoeuvre, rather unreal. Each group did claim to have got something of the 'feel' of the interests of their delegation, and indeed the concrete proposals they had made had shown that this was so. The UFP group were asked if they had known beforehand of the boycott which had occured at the real Conference, and claimed that they had not. They had simply decided, like Welenski, that talking was pointless. The class did not think, however, that the simulation had been pointless. They were interested in repeating the experiment when another suitable topic presented itself. And the teacher was convinced that by and large his objectives had been realized.

Why use simulation in history teaching?

Every practising historian is constantly engaged in some form of simulation. Historians create drama within their own imaginations. The writing of history demands that the writer use his powers of sympathetic imagination as well as his ability to conjure up a picture. An historian may see a place with his mind's eye. But to understand people he has to do more than merely see them. To appreciate motivation, to understand the reactions of actual persons to historical events, he needs to see places, things, and happenings as they saw them, to look imaginatively through their eyes. Historians are hampered in making this imaginative leap, not only by their ignorance of all the relevant facts, but also, paradoxically, by their greater knowledge. They know what happened later. They know the consequences of historical actions in a way that the participants did not. If we want to understand history as it was, rather than as it turned out to be, we have to disengage ourselves from the present and try to live mentally in the past. Why did Chamberlain sacrifice the Czechoslovakian Sudetenland to Hitler in 1938? We know now what Chamberlain did not know then: that this was just one more step in Hitler's march to European hegemony. But how did it look to Chamberlain in 1938? To know that we must simulate the situation of that year and mentally dramatize the meetings between the Prime Minister and the Fuehrer.

Simulation in this sense is an integral part of historical thinking.

Exercises which involve simulation should therefore be an important part of teaching history. In junior classes 'acting history' has for a long time been recognized as a useful teaching method. It has been pointed out that asking pupils to re-enact a scene from their history textbooks is no less relevant to history learning than asking them to write an imaginative letter or to describe the causes and effects of an historical episode.

The simulation exercise described above was a sort of drama, but it was an open-ended drama. The pupils had to assume roles and then instead of acting out the parts, they had to solve an historical problem. This particular technique of teaching is newer than that of simple dramatization and is commonly associated with the training of executives and policy-makers or the creation of roles in social studies, rather than with history learning. But it can be used to great advantage in history lessons, provided that it is realized that the result of the simulation may not necessarily correspond to the historical result. In one published account of a large-scale simulation of the First World War, Germany was eliminated early in the proceedings and Italy was not involved in the fighting at all owing to the distrust of the other nations. But if the simulation has been carried out seriously, history can be learned by a comparison of the simulation result and the real result. What factors in 1914 and 1915 prevented Germany from being eliminated so quickly by larger armies? Simulation may be a lengthy way of teaching historical content. But if it does not primarily teach content, what does it teach? It has always been recognized that drama can help to create interest in an historical topic. This by itself is a limited instructional objective, and it is questionable whether the children are becoming interested in drama or in history. Through drama and through simulation exercises children are encouraged to identify with historical characters. Such identification is a common ingredient in childhood play and adolescent fantasy. If this natural tendency can be harnessed in the study of history it must surely enrich the quality of the learning process. Drama and simulation can also give pupils the sense of the uncertainty of history. This is of course the secret of its dramatic appeal. History was not bound to turn out as it did. Probably none of the characters engaged in historical events guessed accurately how things would turn out. A well structured simulation, like a well written narrative, can take a pupil imaginatively into that atmosphere of doubt, which the effect of hindsight tends to dispel. The exercise of empathy, of sympathetic imagination, also gives pupils an insight into the real essence of historical problems. To understand the problems of the past we need to view them from a number of angles. Insight can be given for example by statistical studies relating to the economic background of an historical event. But without the exercise of empathy there is a danger of assuming that history is determined by factors never considered by the actual participants. Lastly, besides helping pupils to understand historical problems, simulation can give further insight into the problems of history. How can one know what really happened in the past? A catalogue of all the influences that might have been present in an historical situation is not enough. We must be able to put ourselves in the place of the characters we study in order to assess the effects those influences might have had at a given date in a given place. Such conclusions can never be scientifically certain, but that is an inherent feature of the discipline of history, and the sooner our pupils realize this the sooner they will begin to develop historical understanding.

Varieties of drama and simulation in history teaching

Plays
These may either be scripted or unscripted.

Scripted plays   These are most valuable as vehicles of history learning when the scripts have been prepared by the pupils themselves. Turning a narrative description into human speech is a very useful exercise: What sort of language would they have used? What sort of accent? A play which is well rehearsed and performed in costume can give the participants a great deal of enjoyment and involves many aspects of history, since words, dress, and gesture must be related as closely as possible to the historical models. The great pity of such performances is that they are over so quickly and are rarely repeated. The use of tape-recorders may enlarge the scope of scripted history plays. A class may write and perform a radio drama which can then be preserved on tape and used again with another class.

Unscripted plays   These are sometimes known as 'spontaneous drama'. The spontaneity is on the part of the pupils—not on the part of the teacher. While such plays are unrehearsed, they should not be unprepared, and success depends as much on the teacher's preparatory activities as it does in the case of a scripted play. With a simple historical story it is possible for the teacher and the class to plan a script together. The story can be written in brief on the chalkboard and then divided into scenes or acts. Parts are given to the actors and with a knowledge of the story well in mind the pupils can act out the scenes. While perhaps less suitable for public performance, an unscripted play can be a good classroom exercise. But it must be related to the size and environment of the room or organizational difficulties may prevent its success as an instructional experience. The teacher will have to maintain control in order not to emulate the experience of H.M. Madeley's fictitious teacher whose star performer

> 'Acted Brutus to the life,
> And killed Joe Turner with a knife.'

Too much realism sometimes produces problems.

Sociodrama

This term is usually restricted to the type of role-play common in social studies, in which the players seek to solve a social problem by means of simulation. In history teaching it refers to a type of dramatization in which the players are given historical roles and an historical problem or issue and by simulation they pursue the issue to some conclusion in terms of the roles that they are playing. Most published descriptions of 'simulation games', as they are often mistermed, deal with large-scale events, the Berlin Conference, the First World War, and involve activities that go on for days. Monitors and assessors are required to see that the role-players keep to the rules, and where there is a competitive element some system of adjudication has to be built in. Without decrying such ambitious experiments it seems likely that a smaller operation, such as the Lancaster House simulation which lasted a double period, will fit more conveniently into most teachers' schemes of work. The method has one great advantage over scripted or unscripted plays: it is easier to involve boys and girls in the senior school.

Simulation and drama

The problem-solving aspect, the competitive element, and the importance of remaining faithful to the historical situation will convince them that this is more than mere play-acting. The empathetic powers of adolescents are no feebler than those of juniors, even if they may be hidden by that reticence and lack of spontaneity which accompanies some stages of adolescent emotional and physical development.

Debates

This is an older form of sociodrama with set rules and an inherent atmosphere of competition. A debate on an historical topic in which the speakers adopt either the role of a particular historical personality or an historically valid party position can be both stimulating and instructional. A well known variation on this theme is the 'lecturette' given by pupils to their peers and awarded marks by the hearers. This strategy may have dramatic interest if the speakers adopt historical roles and, instead of lecturing *about* Marco Polo, describe what Marco Polo actually saw or felt in the first person.

Gaming

Structured board-games with a high content of simulation have been popular commercially for many years now. It seems that childhood games of 'cops and robbers' or games with lead soldiers and toy forts are replaced in adulthood by games like Monopoly, which make use of social and econmic problems to provide an enjoyable competitive exercise. If 'cops and robbers' has acquired classroom cousins in the forms of plays and sociodrama; toy soldier exercises and Monopoly have also been imitated in instructional experiments. Monopoly can teach its players a lot about real estate, and it is possible to devise board-games to be played with dice and a variety of instruction cards which teach about historical situations. A game called 'Trade and Discovery' has been published and a workshop held at the University of Zambia produced a number of models, including the rather terrifying 'Slave Trade' game. The main purpose of simulation activities is not the acquisition of historical facts so much as an insight into the complexities of historical situations. But do such games have any real value in history classes? It is evident that they have. The complications of trans-oceanic commerce can be built into a board-game like 'Trade and Discovery' in a way that is both interesting and accurate. (The question of taste has to be considered, of course. Human tragedy should not be trivialized: e.g. 'You are caught in a storm. Throw twenty slaves overboard and go back three places.') But given good sense, a reasonably realistic simulation of some historical situations can be reduced to a board and dice. It may be difficult to decide when such games could be played, but a fearless teacher could start them off in class time and hope that pupils will be engrossed enough to continue playing them during recreation.

Instant simulation

Besides the foregoing exercises, which require careful thought and preparation by the teacher, there is room in history teaching for instant simulation of an historical episode. This happens often enough during a teacher's own exposition. Having described the background of an historical situation, he can ask the class or an individual pupil to accept a role and imagine how the events took place: 'If you were Lobengula what would you have done? You cannot read or write. You are interested in firearms to give you power over African neighbours. How would you have reacted to Rudd?'

In this way the process of understanding an historical narrative becomes a series of dramatic experiences in which the historical events, imagined by the pupils, become for a while immediate problems.

Teacher's guide

Research

The dramatization of any historical episode depends for its instructional value on its closeness to the original situation. This closeness is not necessarily a matter of props or costumes but rather of thought and understanding. All simulation and drama requires careful research by the teacher so that the issues that the pupils face

imaginatively are those of the historical past, not something
invented out of a half-understood narrative.

Performance
A simulation exercise which has been adequately researched normally
succeeds instructionally if it does not overstrain the participants or
the environment. You can have a conference in a classroom, you
cannot have the Battle of Bunker's Hill. It is often better to be less
ambitious at the beginning and to temper the imaginative suggestions
of an interested class with some cool common sense. Once in
operation the drama or simulation should be allowed (within the
bounds of safety) to go its own way. Too much interference by the
teacher, hoping to steer the drama along its historical path, will
bring imaginative simulating to a grinding halt. If things do go
'wrong' historically then one can always ask why once the exercise
is over.

Follow-up
A post-mortem analysis of a simulation exercise, if it is done without
carping or personal criticism, can be an important element in the
instructional experience. Comparison of the simulation with the
'real thing' is necessary in the case of sociodrama, otherwise some
pupils may be left thinking that Italy did not fight in the First
World War! In other forms of drama too the differences between
the acted and the original events can be examined, not only to point
out the divergences but also to emphasize the richness of the real
episode. What elements in the real event had to be left out of the
dramatization? And what aspects of the real situation can we only
guess at today?

Exercises

1   Devise a sociodrama on an historical issue. Write policy or
    position statements for each of the characters or groups involved
    in the drama. Make sure that each role-player has enough

knowledge of the situation to enable him to move meaningfully towards a conclusion true to the historical context.

2 Explain in a ten-minute micro-teaching session some episode that involves simulation. Try to get the pupils to continue the narrative by putting themselves in the positions of the historical characters discussed.

3 Teach a practice lesson to a junior secondary form, making use of an unscripted drama to involve the pupils in the historical situation. Your instructional objectives for the lesson should include enabling pupils to feel what it was like to be involved in that particular episode.

Further reading

P.J. Tansey (ed.), *Educational aspects of simulation,* McGraw-Hill (London, 1971).

R.J. Unstead, *Teaching history in the junior school,* A. & C. Black (London, 1969.)

P.J. Tansey and Derick Unwin, *Simulation and gaming in education,* Methuen Educational (London, 1969).

Harry McNicol, *History, heritage and environment,* Faber (London, 1946).

Colin Newcombe, 'Wargames in the classroom' in *Teaching History,* vol. I, No. 4. Historical Association (London, 1970).

G. Milliken, 'Simulation in history teaching: promising innovation or passing fad?' in *Teaching History*, vol. II, No. 7. Historical Association (London, 1971).

Jon Nicol, 'Simulation and history teaching: Trade and Discovery, a history game for use in schools' in *Teaching History,* vol. II, No. 7. Historical Association (London, 1971).

D. Birt and J. Nichol, *Games and simulations in history*, Longmans (London, 1975).

8
Projects

There is an informal air about this lesson. The pupils are seated in
groups, but are not involved in group study. They are listening with
amusement to a spokesman from one group who is reporting on
work done over the last two weeks.

'Then the man in the office said that we would have to apply to
the Prime Minister's office.'

The thought of a bedraggled bunch of schoolboys arriving on the
P.M.'s doormat causes some giggles.

'But didn't he say whether there had been any information issued
to the public or published in any form?'

'No, he said that there was a security blanket, and that neither he
nor any of his staff could talk to us without authorization from the
Prime Minister's office.'

'So what are you going to do next?'

'We don't know. Do you think the school could get us permission
from the Prime Minister?'

'I doubt if that could be done quickly enough.' (The teacher is
speaking.) 'Even if the Head thought it worth trying, we need to
have the project completed by the end of term and it would take till
then to get an answer through the channels which lead to and from
the Prime Minister. Can anyone else suggest what this group should
do now?'

'What about the newspaper offices?'

'Yes, that is a good idea. There must have been a lot in the press
at one time or another, and to get it you do not even have to go to
the newspaper offices. You can find back numbers in the city library
if you ask them. Do you know what date the hall was opened? You
need to work backwards and forwards from that date. Backwards
to find all about the plans and the hopes and difficulties encountered.

103

Forwards, to investigate the ways in which the place has actually been used. You have already got one big question to answer on this topic. Can anyone tell us what it is?'

'Why is there a security blanket?'

'Yes, but I would not try too hard to answer it if I were you. Keep a look-out for the answer, but don't make it an open objective or you may run into further security problems.'

This group had chosen to investigate the story of the city's large convention hall as part of a local history project. Used for everything from major international political conferences to 'all-star wrestling', the hall was thought to have a story worth investigating. Unfortunately no one had been willing to help the pupil-investigators, and they had finally been told that no information was available for security reasons. Thus the search for alternative sources of information and the almost inevitable suggestion of the local press had arisen.

Most of the other groups had got further in the first fortnight of their efforts. The team examining the big medical complex outside the city had found plenty of official co-operation and had used the excuse that it was founded early to justify their concentration of effort on the nurses' school! The local airport manager had also been helpful, although that group seemed to have spent more time enjoying hospitality than acquiring information. At the suburban 'site-and-service' housing scheme, the organizers had been delighted with the interest of the young investigators and had lined up a series of interviews for them.

The first report of the groups' activities was of course merely a check on the progress of their researches. While one team needed encouragement and the suggestion of new resources, others needed assistance in selecting one area out of several likely possibilities. Each group then had to try to identify a theme that might be worth following, so that their further investigation would begin to have a definite shape. This was not possible in every case, since there was not yet enough information from some groups to suggest a line of approach. But by the end of the period each team had to some extent modified its programme of investigations and taken part in the re-shaping of those of other groups. There would not now be another project lesson until the pupils had completed the bulk of their information-finding, possibly in three or four weeks' time.

Projects

Objectives

The teacher's aims in this fairly unstructured exercise were, firstly,
to make sure that all the groups were active (and to give the right
sort of encouragement to those that were not), and secondly, to get
the pupil-investigators to ask questions about the information they
had acquired, and to prevent their knowledge becoming a mere
catalogue of facts by shaping it into an explanation or narrative.

Public reporting helped the achievement of the first objective.
While some teams had interview reports on which to work already,
others, like the group which visited the airfield, were embarrassed
at their own lack of solid findings. A date had been fixed for the
end of the 'research' and the beginning of the 'writing-up' period,
and the lazier teams had begun to realize how much work they still
had to do to reach the target on schedule.

The limiting factor of a date for the end of investigations made
the shaping of the individual projects by the establishment of a
definite line of approach very important. Each topic had some
problem to be solved. Security at the convention hall was obviously
one of them. ('Are the wrestling matches rigged?' was one pertinent
question.) The continued existence of the tiny town airfield
apparently unconnected with the international aerodrome outside
the city suggested a line of questioning there. What is the object of
a 'site-and-service' scheme and how does it work in a city like this?
In a new city local history research tends to be 'contemporary' in
outlook and relates the recent past to present or even future needs.
But the pupils were free to find the theme of their topics from
their own experiences in the preliminary investigation: the emphasis
on contemporary purpose was determined by the nature of the
establishments they were examining.

What use are history projects?

The lesson described above concerned a project in local history.
There are obviously many other types of project possible in history
learning and an attempt to categorize them will be made in the
following section. Here we are concerned with the concept of a project

105

as an investigatory activity carried out by schoolchildren in the study of an historical subject.

Projects may either be individual assignments or organized in teams. They can relate mainly to secondary or mainly to primary source material. But they are alike in that they give the pupil a large amount of freedom in selecting a topic for investigation, in pursuing it through the available resources with a minimum of teacher supervision, and in presenting the findings as the results of personal or group research.

Professional writers of history have been known to deride the introduction of research activities into the school curriculum, mainly on the grounds that these activities are not 'real' research and do not contribute to the development of future historians. History teachers should not be worried by definitions of research and should not be concerned if none of their pupils make it into the Stubbs or Namier class. History projects are a means of educating the minds and enriching the cultural experience of pupils. If it is valid to make use of the discipline of history for general educational purposes, then it is also quite legitimate to use the methods and techniques of historical investigation for the same end.

But what special advantages can a project or investigation bring to history learning? It is sometimes claimed that project work makes history lessons more interesting. Unfortunately this is not necessarily true. While we agree with Sheila Ferguson that 'many children reveal unsuspected ability and interests when they are able to work at their own speed on their own subject', many teachers will also encounter pupils who never voluntarily choose any topic. For some pupils a project is even less palatable than rote or textbook learning simply because it involves them in much harder work; in thinking for themselves and organizing their own study programme.

Here we are closer to the true value of the project method in history and in other subjects. Many of our exercises in history teaching are modes by which we train pupils to study by themselves. The project is another stage in this process, calling for greater initiative on the pupils' part, while giving them freedom to choose their own topic and organize their investigations themselves, although they can always ask the teacher to help if necessary.

A history project both calls for and exercises the pupils in a series of interconnected study skills. The seeking of information, the formulation of hypotheses, the use of imagination in selecting the lines of inquiry, the extraction of relevant material and distinguishing between less important and more important information, the evaluation and checking of evidence, the organization of findings in a sequence based on an established chronology or some other organizational principle; all these skills are necessary for the professional historian. But they should also be part of the intellectual repertoire of any educated person. Carefully structured projects carried out in secondary schools can therefore have real educational value.

However, while through a history project schoolchildren can obtain experience of a variety of mental activities, the total experience should add up to more than the sum of its parts. With guidance from a teacher, pupils obtain insight into the way in which history is put together, begin to appreciate the role of the historian in the making of history, learn to identify subjectivity and bias, and analyse the importance of the types of source material used. They begin to realize through projects that there is a difference between written history and the probable happenings of the past. They face the problems of conflicting evidence or lack of evidence, and they will be introduced to different types of evidence and have to consider their validity. None of these realizations will be carried to great depths and many pupils will barely notice what would seem obvious to an intelligent adult. But if by participation in a school-based project adolescents begin to develop a slightly more critical approach to historical writing, the method will have proved its worth both as a tool for history teaching and for general education.

The project method of teaching undoubtedly has its difficulties. It involves hard work for both the pupils and the teacher. The problem of the lazy or insufficiently motivated pupil is emphasized in a learning experience which depends so much on personal effort. And the difficulties of finding realistic research topics related to resources which are locally available can often be solved only by a combination of toil and imagination. But an efficient teacher can overcome them and can guide his pupils to conduct a worthwhile investigation, while giving them an enjoyable and valuable educational experience.

Variety of school history projects

The term 'project' has been used to mean many different things in educational literature. It is frequently thought of as an inter-disciplinary concentration on a single area of study for several days or weeks: for instance, the science, geography, art, history, and even literature departments may combine to study the local river. The word 'project' is also used in practical subjects to mean a specific behavioural task given in the course of the ordinary curriculum, e.g. in a woodwork class each pupil may be required to make a coffee table by the end of the term. In this book the word 'project' is used to mean an investigation, undertaken individually or by teams of children, in which the participants are given considerable freedom in their choice of a topic, mode of approach, execution of research, and presentation of their findings.

There are two main types of investigatory projects practised in secondary schools:

1   *Book-based projects*   This refers to the personal study of a topic in library or archival sources, both within and outside the school. The source material may be primary or secondary in nature, and the project may last anything from a few days to a term or longer. Some of the projects suggested by Sheila Ferguson (see 'Further reading' section) can only be done through secondary sources. The number of topics possible for any class will depend on the size of the library or the availability of ancillary resources near a particular school.

There are two difficulties to be overcome in this sort of investigation. First, how much of it should derive from the pupil's own initiative and how much should be directed by the teacher? Obviously, if the teacher simply tells the pupil what to read then the aspect of personal investigation disappears. If on the other hand a teacher limits his assistance to criticism of what has already been done by the pupil, his role as a guide will be lost. Perhaps class discussion on the topics, resulting in suggestions both from the teacher and from other pupils, can provide guidance which does not become direction.

Secondly, there is a danger that pupils may copy long passages of material out of books without understanding them. It should be established that direct quotations must relate to argument, and that there will be no praise for including irrelevant material. One suggestion that has been made is that each of the headings or sub-headings in a project report should be in the form of a question. Then the relevance of the material gathered will be easier to control.

2 *Field-based projects* The study of local history invites pupils to look at resources outside the libraries or local archives. Local people are a valuable source of evidence if the topic is recent enough. The pupils' own families often provide both worthwhile and accessible information. Similarly, buildings, machinery, excavated sites, or ruins invite investigation simply by being there. The value of local history both as a study and a source of learning has been reiterated by teachers and historians over the last forty years. Local study brings history home to the pupils. It helps them to see that ordinary things as well as extraordinary things have a past. It gives a schoolchild an opportunity to investigate things that no one has studied before: in short to be a pioneer in history. It can also act as a stepping-stone to an understanding of wider historical topics which have had an influence on local circumstances. As a school exercise, historical investigation involving field-work shows pupils that history, although it tends to be more book-bound than many other subjects, is not merely about books but about people and the way they have organized their communal living over the ages.

Besides these main forms of project, there are other school activities which are closely related to them:

3 *Structured visits* The local museum or a local site of known historical interest can provide useful material for pupils to investigate. In these cases however the research is modified by the structure of the establishment in which the resources are preserved. Pupils may of course make use of museums in a straightforward local history project. Often museum visiting is used simply as an excuse to get children out of the classroom, and sometimes it is even made an end in itself, as if teachers should be commended for the number of museum visits their charges have made. To be a meaningful and

instructional exercise, a museum visit should be seen as a means and not an end: a means to learning something quite definite about the past that was not known before. The teacher should therefore give his pupils a specific task to perform during the museum visit, and that task should be related to the normal curriculum of the class. Many museums nowadays have educational services which supply questionnaires and other devices for structuring the work of pupil visitors. Teachers can make use of these to organize more precise and relevant investigatory tasks for their own pupils.

4   *Short project tasks*   Besides major investigation assignments which may take the pupils three weeks of concentrated effort or be spread over a term or longer, it is often possible and always useful to give children short opportunities for personal investigation within certain topic areas of the regular curriculum. Family history, for example, can be examined by means of a single well-devised questionnaire. And where the teacher's own knowledge is deficient, as it may be in cross-cultural situations (e.g. in schools with a high immigrant intake) or in places where cultural history has not yet been professionally studied (as in some developing countries) pupils are capable of making a real contribution as they ferret out information from relatives and neighbours about village organizations, kinship systems, and other social aspects of a locality's past. A single sheet of questions can provide pupils with matter for a couple of evenings' investigation and enrich subsequent lessons with individual interpretation of the topic under study.

Teacher's guide

Organization of projects

Preparation   The teacher must decide whether a project should be undertaken by individual pupils or by groups. For field studies, local history, etc., groups of four to six children are often advisable. On the other hand work during museum visits is best done individually.

The teacher should also draw up a list of possible topics within the general theme or area of the proposed project. Although this method demands some freedom of choice on the part of the pupil-investigators, that freedom will inevitably be curtailed by circumstances. This means of course that the teacher should obtain some background information before the pupils begin their research. This is especially useful in field studies. Had the teacher done a little more homework for the lesson described above, his charges would not have wasted time trying to run round a security blanket.

When project work is being done in the classroom, the teacher should see that the class furniture is arranged suitably for group or informal teaching.

Procedure　The following list describes one possible way of setting up a secondary school project:

a)　If the investigation is to be done in teams, the class is first divided into groups of four to six pupils.

b)　The individuals or teams then select topics, usually from a list of 'possibles' presented by the teacher.

c)　The children then draw up a few questions (not more than six) through which they begin to investigate their topic. These are guidelines for their first attempts at data collection and their formulation will probably require some help from the teacher.

d)　Pupils then list the sources from which they hope to obtain the information demanded by their own questions.

e)　According to a timetable determined beforehand, the individuals or teams then undertake their first investigations.

f)　A report on the first inquiries is made, after which a fresh set of questions is drawn up for the next stage of research. This process of inquiry and reporting can be repeated as many times as are necessary for the project as a whole.

g)　Having drawn up a final report on their findings, the pupils then organize it in order to communicate it to the rest of the class. This is often done be preparing a booklet (within, say, manila folders) or by creating some sort of display, with a bulletin board, models, charts, etc.

h)　It is usually worthwhile, either before or after the communication of findings, to hold an evaluatory exercise with the participants. The teacher tries to assess what benefit the class

111

derived from the investigations other than the acquisition of the information which they have included in their final report.

Difficulties inherent in the method

Timetabling   Field studies and even library research cannot conveniently be done using only the single periods of the scheduled history lessons. Double periods give greater scope, but if pupils are to leave the school premises, it is advisable to ask permission for a whole afternoon to be devoted to the project occasionally.

Transport   Field work demands transport to and from the area being studied. This can cause difficulties both for rural and urban schools. The teacher should consider transport possibilities when listing research topics. For a local study the teacher should investigate the area adjacent to the school in the hope of finding enough interesting subjects within walking or cycling distance.

Lack of topics   It is easy for a teacher to conclude that the locality and other resources do not provide enough topics of interest or value if he is looking for something large, ambitious, or historically romantic. School projects need to be very small in scale to fit the time usually available and the speed of the investigators. Thus instead of a whole town or village, the history of one shop, one local government department, or one site can provide enough scope for a project.

Pupil apathy   This can be very discouraging to the teacher, especially when 'the books' say that projects should arouse interest. But apathy must have a reason and unless that reason is discovered it will continue. A lazy child may be placed in a group of enthusiasts in the hope that some of their keenness may rub off on him. But if the apathy derives from a lack of self-confidence resulting from some emotional problem, an individual project rather than a team project may be more suitable. In normal circumstances, interest in a project results from two inter-related factors: the teacher's own enthusiasm for the exercise and his efficiency in planning and organizing one within the capabilities of the pupils he is instructing.

Projects

Exercises

1   Draw up a list of local history topics which can be investigated
    in your area, with an outline of resources available for each
    topic. Estimate the number of hours of investigation, reporting,
    and writing-up that a team of secondary pupils would require to
    complete each topic.
2   Write a questionnaire to assist pupils to investigate an historical
    topic either in a local museum or at a nearby historical site.
    Arrange the questions in a suitable sequence.
3   In a teaching practice session, organize a small library-based
    project on a variety of topics within the scope of the syllabus
    you are teaching. Organize the results of the pupils' investigations
    so that the information collected is communicated to all
    members of the class.

Further reading

Tom Corfe (ed.), *History in the field,* Blond Educational (London,
    1970).
The Schools Council, *The Certificate of Secondary Education:
    The place of the personal topic: history*, H.M.S.O. (London,
    1968).
Sheila Ferguson, *Projects in history for the secondary school,*
    Batsford (London, 1967).
M.S. Dilke (ed.), *Field studies for schools,* Rivingtons (London,
    1965).
Margaret E. Bryant, *The museum and the school,* Historical
    Association (London, 1961).

9

Communicating history

A group of pupils is seated with the teacher around a large table.
Each child has cartridge paper, pencils, and a ruler. Some have other
drawing instruments: compasses, etc. Propped up in front or
lying nearby each pupil is a copy of a class textbook and they are all
studying a photograph bearing the caption: 'A gold mine in South
Africa, 1890'.

Two of the boys are attempting to sketch part of the photograph. The others are discussing with the teacher exactly what the
picture shows.

'That trolley with two wheels standing on a slant—is it for bringing
something to the ledge or taking something away?'

'Perhaps it is for tipping waste into the valley.'

'What about the man with the basin, what is he doing?'

'He must be "panning", although I am not sure what that
means.'

'Does anyone know what prospectors do when they "pan"? . . .'

'Someone had better look it up in an encyclopedia. We want as
full an explanation as possible, because it may give us a clue what
those other bits and pieces are for.'

'Those frames for instance—there is something that resembles a
large catapult. Is it joined to this trolley rail at the front of the
picture?'

This is the only representation of an early gold mine that the class
has been able to find. This team are trying to interpret it in detail
because the photograph is to be the source of information for a
three-dimensional model of an early South African mine. The
source has to be accurate, therefore nothing could be better than an
actual photograph. But before they can make a model which really
represents history 'as it was' they have to establish exactly what

114

each part of the picture means. They are going to be using other skills later in the exercise. But at the moment they are not yet concerned with the problems of handicraft that the model building is going to present.

Objectives

This team has chosen the gold mine out of a list of possible subjects for study under the heading 'Industry and Society in South and Central Africa'. The teacher has decided that the best way to get his pupils to look at the close details of some aspect of that part of his history syllabus is to ask them to produce a three-dimensional model of some site or object related to the topic. He is not concerned so much with the artistry of the finished product as with the historical interpretation of the original source. All the teams have to work from photographs or plans, and they have to use them in a strictly functional way, so that each model really looks like something that may once have had a use.

How does creative communication contribute to history learning?

History as we know it is the expression in the present of some aspect of the past. Some historians belittle their own role and describe history as the past expressing itself in some way to the present. This expression may be the mute existence of a relic, a document, or an artefact. But it is only meaningful if its historical significance is understood. Thus the photograph that the team were studying was just a photograph of men, simple machines, stones, and boulders. Only when the pupils began to think of it as historical data surviving from the early days of South African gold mining did it become an expression of the past to the present.

While the relics of the past are undoubtedly true and objective in themselves, they do not contribute to history until they are placed within an historical context by a human mind. And when the human mind does this it makes use of a conception of the past for which the surviving relic becomes an example or a piece of evidence.

History is more than simply the left-overs of the past. It is the explanation of those left-overs, their synthesis in a narrative which gives the past a meaning. This act of explanation is the creative work of the historian, for the relics of history are not like a jig-saw puzzle in which every piece eventually finds its place. They are more like the contents of a box of odd pieces, and it is often difficult to see whether all the pieces belong to one puzzle or to several. The historian's art is to produce meaning from a jumble of evidence, to create order out of what sometimes resembles chaos. And to teach pupils (at various levels) to create such order is to train them in a basic historical skill.

There are many ways of expressing or communicating an explanation of the past. We spend so much time reading history books that we tend to feel that the only way to communicate history is to write about it. But many historians use other ways of telling their stories. A museum for example may mount an exhibition to describe the French Revolution or the Battle of Britain or the building of the Canadian Pacific Railway. In this case the historian collects documents, models, photographs, etc. and arranges them in a display which effectively tells the story. Other historians use television as a medium and represent history by means of films, still photographs, interviews and reminiscences, which they synthesize into a form of historical narrative. Historical creativity is an act of synthesis, which turns the results of minute study into a comprehensible whole.

Many teachers will admit that they learnt more history once they began actually to teach it than when they were studying it full-time at college. This is not surprising. Teaching history is in itself a creative activity. It requires powers of synthesis to organize both historical evidence and the activities of a group of pupils into an effective learning experience. When we are forced to synthesize we often realize how shallow some of our own analysis has been, and so, rather than give a bad lesson, we go back to the sources, improve our knowledge, and fill the gaps.

Most of the pupils mentioned in the lesson described above had seen that photograph in their textbooks before. For many of them it had made no special impression. It is actually rather a dull photograph, showing more dust than anything else—not a romantic representation of prospecting for precious minerals. But once given a creative task, that of making a three-dimensional representation of an early mine, the pupils were obliged to use the picture for analysis and interpretation. In the making of the model, in the act of synthesis, they would discover how satisfactory their attempts at analysis and interpretation had been.

Various ways of expressing or communicating history

Writing

Imaginative writing   For many years the formal essay was the traditional fashion of schoolchildren's historical writing, but it is now accepted that before the 'certificate year', which is often the fourth or fifth year of secondary studies, attempts to develop formal essay writing habits can be counterproductive. And now that the teaching of history at post-primary levels affects a wider range of pupils than that produced by selective streaming into strictly academic schools or forms, teachers have had to look for other types of writing more compatible with the intellectual development of less 'literary' children. Several kinds have been successfully tried.

a)   *Script writing*   The writing of a script for a play or a taped radio drama is a good exercise in imagination and synthesis, because it is concerned almost entirely with the writing of direct speech. Other aspects have to be considered as well —props, or noises off, etc.—but the main business of turning a story into life-like speech may interest pupils who show little ability in other forms of writing.

b)   *News-sheets or historical journalism*   A news-sheet created for an historical period is another way of getting children to use their imaginations in history. The events of a particular day or week can be summed up in a striking headline by pupils who would find a three-page essay very difficult. Again, non-literary material can be included: cartoons, illustrations, lay-outs. All these add interest to what is basically an exercise in writing. A production of the 'Paris Courier' for 14th July 1793, with gruesome headlines about the discovery in Marat's bath, is of course an anachronistic exercise. But so is any simulation, and this is a simulated rather than a real paper. Only if pupils really believe that the eighteenth-century press greatly resembled the modern dailies is there a danger of anachronistic thinking in history, and a good teacher will not allow that to happen.

c)   *Eye-witness accounts or letters*   The writing of a letter or an eye-witness account in the name and person of an historical character is a valuable exercise in empathy and historical synthesis. In composing a letter from a soldier at the Ypres front in 1916 to his mother at home, the pupil is obliged to 'feel' the emotions and the dangers of the trenches before he puts them down in written form. In this sort of activity anachronism must be carefully avoided (the weapons must belong to the right war!). The success of a child in avoiding anachronism is a very effective measure of his comprehension of the historical situation.

Short descriptive writing   A description given as an 'eye-witness account' is obviously subjective, although it may be true to the period or topic. When children can stand away from an historical incident and write an account that is both balanced and complete they have reached a further stage in developing true historical creativity. It is best done gradually and on a small scale. A paragraph describing an event or a character is a testing assignment in summing up the knowledge acquired from a lesson or the pages of a book. Children must be taught to write their ideas in their own words, and an exercise in summarizing prevents plagiarism. If this begins to resemble the traditional 'précis writing' of the English course, it is not necessarily a bad thing, for the ability to extract the essence of an argument or description, analyse it, and synthesize it in a clear and concise way is as useful for the writer of history as for anyone else.

A necessary preliminary to the writing of a short passage based on scattered information is the preparation of notes. Pupils should be taught to collect their information in note form before they decide on the shape and extent of the paragraph. Writing from their own notes rather than directly from the sources is a further guarantee that pupils will present their finished products in a fresh and original form of words.

The narrative or explanatory essay   School examinations, especially at the end of secondary education, have long been dominated by the essay. The place of the essay as a means of assessment in history will be discussed in Part 2 of this book. Here we are concerned with the essay as a means of learning history rather than of re-gurgitating it. But teachers are obliged in practice to think of the essay in its normal examination length. In theory there is no historical reason why a pupil should not write five hundred pages on the causes of the Crimean War rather than five pages, but teachers have to read what their pupils write and are therefore usually quite satisfied that their essays should be of examination length.

At secondary level most essays tend to be descriptive. They are concerned either with a description of events or an account of a form of analysis which has usually been learnt by rote. 'Explain the causes of the First World War' is no more explanatory in form than 'Describe the events which led to the First World War'. Even at sixth-form level, where essay questions may demand an original slant, the commonest type of essay is a description with either an introduction or a final paragraph which has some connection with the wording of the title. In secondary schools most pupils are not yet ready to make an original analysis of historical data, and the skill of writing a long piece of accurate historical description is difficult enough to justify the time spent on teaching it.

One major problem in pupils' essays is that of relevance. The content of an essay must relate to the title or question given by the teacher. If pupils introduce unusually large sections of irrelevant material into their work it is either because they have not sufficiently mastered the content to realize what is relevant and what is not, or because they have not acquired the technique of abstracting from a mass of data material which pertains to the topic in which they are interested. Here the preparation of essay notes is a vital exercise. Before writing an essay plan pupils should first assemble notes relevant to the topic from the various sources available. If any pupil has obvious difficulties in writing relevantly he or she can be given a separate assignment: to write notes from a textbook or other source relevant to the title of an essay.

Once the relevant material has been assembled it has to be put into the proper essay form. Here the commonest mistakes are verbosity, which tends to prevent the completion of examination essays with a time limit, and lack of logical order. Both can be partly corrected in the planning stage. Notes, once assembled, should be rearranged in the order in which the essay will be written. If there are four, five, or six items in the answer to the question, then four, five, or six paragraphs will have to be written. In making an essay plan the pupil collects the note material and organizes it into those paragraphs. He then decides if he needs an introductory section or a conclusion, and he has the skeleton of a concise history essay. How can he go wrong?

Well, the very act of rearrangement is a pitfall for many pupils. Some are slow, so they prefer to save time by writing the essay without a plan, usually with very chaotic results. Others have very little problem with organizing the plan, but have difficulty in sticking to it. Both faults can be overcome only with practice and with the careful guidance of the teacher.

One of the most important factors in improving a pupil's essay writing is the teacher's ability to diagnose a fault and give the correct advice to overcome it. The teacher's guidance is therefore very important. Some teachers even write 'model' essays for their pupils to imitate. It may be good for schoolchildren to see a really excellent essay once in a while just to set a high standard, although a very good example produced by a pupil may be more easily emulated than the efforts of an adult teacher. Published collections of 'model answers' should be avoided since the standard they set is rarely what a good teacher would like to see his pupils imitating. However, to plagiarize someone else's essays is no better than plagiarizing a textbook. It is not learning how to write. Other teachers rewrite whole paragraphs of the pupils' efforts and then make them write a fair copy. Rewriting can occasionally help as a guide, but it is better to point out where the paragraph has gone wrong and make the pupil correct it for himself. In the end the only way to learn how to write is to write.

Comments in the margin of an essay are the best way for a teacher to help a pupil improve his work. And for this reason the comments should be constructive. There may be a great temptation to write 'Rubbish' in large red letters alongside a statement, but it is much more useful to write 'Is this relevant?' or 'Is there any evidence for this?' Finally, we must beware of putting pupils into a straitjacket. An essay is a personal thing. There are invariably several ways of organizing and writing it. The teacher's job is to make sure that it conforms to the principles of accuracy, relevance, and logic. If that is done within the limits of an examination-length essay, then it should be regarded as a success.

Graphic work

Graphs, charts, and diagrams   Pupils in modern schools tend to be much more familiar than their parents with mathematical and quasi-mathematical forms of communicating knowledge. Long before the graph has been studied in mathematics lessons, children have been exposed to diagrammatic ways of expressing trends and relationships. 'Modern maths', making greater use as it does of shape and area to delineate number, has considerably improved understanding of information presented in this form. History books nowadays make considerable use of such methods to communicate information, especially numerical information. Figure 10 gives three ways of showing the religious composition of the Indian population in the 1930s. To express a trend some form of histogram can frequently be used as effectively as an ordinary graph.

Pupils with a strong mathematical background are likely to be much more adept at this type of communication than some of their history teachers. They should be encouraged both to turn information into mathematical forms where it is possible to do so and to devise ways of communicating history through mathematical or quasi-mathematical media.

Informative maps   The usefulness of exercises in which pupils have to put historical information on to maps has already been mentioned in the section dealing with map-work (pp. 88-9). This method of communicating history requires the synthesis of both historical and geographical knowledge as well as the exercise of cartographic skills. All pupils need to know how to read historical maps. Pupils who are adept at making them have another means of expressing history at their command.

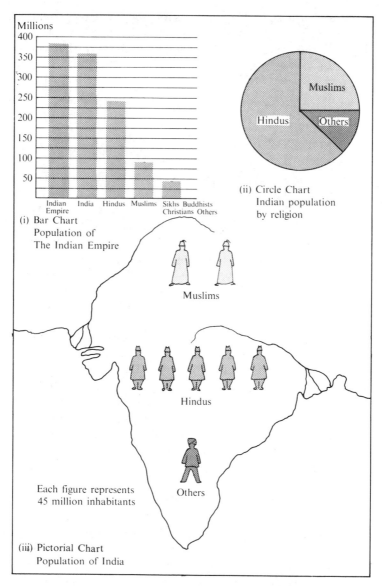

(i) Bar Chart
Population of
The Indian Empire

(ii) Circle Chart
Indian population
by religion

Muslims

Hindus

Others

Each figure represents
45 million inhabitants

(iii) Pictorial Chart
Population of India

Figure 10   Three diagrams: population of India by religion
10(i)   From *Britain and the world in the twentieth century*,
by G.K. Tull and P. Bulwer, Blandford Press (1971).

Displays and exhibitions Maps, diagrams, and charts are all ways of communicating historical information, but each by itself, like the single paragraph, can only express a limited amount. To narrate a whole story several of them need to be connected logically and (because this is graphic work) artistically. While it is not reasonable to expect an individual pupil to produce a 'one-man exhibition' for homework, a team or group might well combine their talents to express a single historical theme or topic. Drawing, friezes, lettering of various kinds, and other artistic techniques can be used to link the major items of information in a logical sequence. This sort of activity can, for example, be a satisfactory conclusion to a local history project, for it enables the pupils to make use of some of the resources they have used for the project as part of the presentation of their findings. If a teacher feels hampered by his own artistic limitations, the talents of his pupils and the advice of colleagues more adept at such things than himself should be sought.

Craft work

Historical uses The making of historical models has long been a favourite activity in primary classrooms and in the junior forms of secondary schools. Sometimes models are made by the teacher and sometimes by the pupils, but the purpose is usually to provide for the students a three-dimensional visual aid for their history lessons. Unfortunately, many models are not very useful as visual aids. Even the professional examples in museums tend to give an air of childish representation to what should be an adult theme. In the age of the film and the still photograph two-dimensional pictures are closer to the original and often more easily comprehended by the pupil. Is there then any valid place in history teaching for the construction of dioramas, scale models, and other representations which require expertise in craft skills as well as historical knowledge and interest?

There are two legitimate objectives for such work in the history lesson: to provide an exercise in historical problem-solving, and to allow an expression of historical understanding.

To construct a model from a cut-out kit or commercial package will not provide children with great scope for problem-solving in history. The teacher may ask questions about the function of the spars and point out the purposes of the various sails, but the *Santa Maria* can be assembled without any questions being asked at all. If on the other hand the pupils are asked to take part in the design as well as in the construction of the model, then they will have to do some historical thinking. In turning the knowledge they have acquired from a written or a pictorial source into a three-dimensional representation they are obliged to interpret closely the sources they are using. Models made by pupils will probably have to be simplified. Pupils should therefore be encouraged to aim at a model that will clearly show the function of the original. Deciding what can be left out is an important act of interpretation. Even if the finished model does not prove of any great assistance to others as a visual aid, the exercise of turning historical knowledge into that form is a useful experiment in translation.

The completed product is a synthesis of the children's knowledge on a certain topic, and the value of the synthesis often depends on the theme chosen for the model. A representation of the Zimbabwe ruins as they appear today will synthesize knowledge of a purely physical nature. To design a model of Zimbabwe as it might have been in A.D. 1400 requires historical reasoning as well as careful examination of the ruins.

A diorama is essentially a functional type of model and is no less difficult to produce because it is only partially three-dimensional. A street in Shakespeare's London will sum up a great deal of knowledge about social history of that period, if buildings, costumes, carriages, etc. are constructed with sufficient authenticity.

Teacher's guide to modelling   For many teachers the construction of models in the classroom seems a more daunting exercise than the drawing of charts and diagrams. Again, the assistance of pupils and colleagues can be harnessed if the objective is thought worthwhile. The history teacher must decide on suitable methods for producing a three-dimensional representation.

a)   *Paper cut-outs*   Periodicals such as *Pictorial Education* issue models for cutting and assembling. This system is perhaps the cleanest of model-making techniques, but it does have the fault of leaving little to the initiative of the pupils. The design of a cut-out model on the other hand would severely tax the draughtsmanship of all but the most gifted children or teachers.

b) *Plasticine or local clay*   Clay is very suitable for modelling buildings, hills, and landscapes. It is difficult to colour, but plasticine can be purchased in a variety of shades, although it is more expensive than clay.

c) *Papier mâché*   Perhaps the messiest of all modelling materials, papier mâché has the advantage of being the most adaptable. It can be cheaply made from old newspapers, and models made from it can be painted easily and preserved when dry.

d) *Household debris*   Harry S. Sutton has devised an entire system of model-making using discarded household objects including detergent packets, plastic bottles, paper straws, and polythene meat trays (see 'Further reading' section). The method calls for good organization of the materials and for imagination in their use. The standardization in size of household containers makes the building of scale models much easier, and some astonishingly realistic models can be produced from the most prosaic materials.

Dramatic representation

To act out an historical role within its proper context is an exercise of the synthesis of physical as well as intellectual skills and historical knowledge. The techniques have been dealt with earlier on pp. 97-101. Combined with imaginative script writing, historical dramatization can be highly instructive and enjoyable both for secondary school pupils and teachers.

Exercises

1 a) Take a typical Ordinary Level essay question. Write notes from a suitable book on the topic of the question. Then rearrange the notes into the form of an essay. Finally, write a short essay, following your plan strictly.

   b) Design three imaginative writing exercises, not including

a formal essay. Do one of the exercises yourself and then write down:
  (i) what new ideas on the topic you gained from doing the exercise;
  (ii) what further information you would have liked in order to make a more satisfactory attempt at imagining the past within the scope of your exercise.
  c) Conduct a discussion with a class in which:
  (i) a set of notes for an essay topic is agreed on;
  (ii) an essay plan is communally worked out from previously prepared notes.
  The writing of the prepared essay can be given to the pupils as a homework assignment.
2 a) In a micro-teaching exercise, ask a group of pupils to design some diagrams or charts to express the information given in one paragraph of a textbook.
  b) At the end of a unit of lessons on a well defined topic, discuss with the class the design of an exhibition to communicate to others the story of the topic, The aim is to use mainly visual material with a minimum of written narrative.
3 Make a three-dimensional model using as a source a picture or a plan of a building or site. Then list:
  a) the difficulties encountered in interpreting the source for the purpose of model-making;
  b) the new information obtained from examination of the source while planning or building the model;
  c) what other information you would need about the original picture or plan in order to be able to express it adequately in the form of a model.

Further reading

John A. Fairley, *Activity methods in history,* Nelson (London, 1967).
E. Milliken and R.E. Crookall, *Historical model making for African schools,* University of London Press (London, 1967).
P.H.J.H. Gosden and D.W. Sylvester, *History for the average child,* Basil Blackwell (Oxford, 1969).
Harry S. Sutton, *Models in action,* Evans Brothers (London 1972).

10
The history teacher

The teacher as historian

Many readers normally confine their concept of the professional historian to the academic researcher and the writer of history books. But although most secondary school history teachers do not usually find time for writing historical monographs, they do nevertheless make their living by history. It is assumed that they have an enduring interest in the subject, and most history teachers consider it part of their professional obligation to keep abreast of the main developments in their field by reading academic and popular historical journals and current publications in the particular areas they are teaching. Fortunately, most teachers think of this as an enjoyable part of their professional duties.

As long as the role of the history teacher was to impart knowledge of historical 'facts', the reading of history books was probably sufficient to keep him informed of new knowledge and to maintain a commitment to historical study. However, as soon as the teacher is expected to instruct his pupils in 'historical thinking' it becomes necessary for him to be constantly involved not just in reading historical books but in practising all aspects of historical thinking, including the creative thinking of the research historian. If pupils are to learn history by 'doing it', then the teacher must keep himself professionally fit by 'doing it' too.

This means of course that the teacher should be involved in some type of historical research. What type of research will depend on the resources and the time available. Some teachers may be able to enroll in post-graduate courses. Others may be able to participate in research teams or even start their own small projects. But the easiest and perhaps the most enjoyable way for a history teacher to become involved in normal historical research is by organizing or participating in a school or community history club. Many communities have a rich variety of written records on local affairs which can be profitably investigated, and in those where written accounts are lacking it would be a valuable exercise to record the stories of older members of the community while they are still alive. Some developing countries have few written sources for their history and cannot afford the professional manpower to undertake the work of recording valuable oral traditions, work which is not seen as directly productive. A school or community history club can render an important service in filling this gap. Furthermore a school history club can add an interesting dimension to the social and intellectual life of a community in any kind of society by investigating the story of a local church, farm, village, etc., and then writing it up in a booklet or making a display or exhibition for the public. Such activities will require considerable commitment from an interested teacher, but despite their amateur status they may produce very worthwhile results: encouraging the historical development of the participants and possibly contributing to academic scholarship.

Expounding history

One typical image of a 'professional' historian is the lecturer or teacher who expounds his historical knowledge in universities or other colleges. While there is no intrinsic reason for one type of history teaching to be more professional than another, it is a fact of academic life that many writers of history books actually earn their living by giving lectures. Should a secondary school teacher who is anxious to absorb the structure of the discipline by conforming to professional behaviour therefore imitate the college lecturer in his own teaching methods? The only possible answer is 'No'.

Some readers may have looked in vain through this book for the expository model of history teaching. But the word 'exposition' describes not so much a learning activity for pupils as a habit of the teacher, and we have insisted on regarding teaching as a means of assisting pupils to learn, rather than as a way of providing satisfactory activities for a teacher. Furthermore, a teacher's exposition cannot stand on its own in a secondary school classroom in the way that it is made to do in a university lecture hall. It should also be remembered that the appropriateness of the lecture as a teaching method is under critical investigation in colleges and universities too.

Within the context of a problem-solving approach to history learning, the best that a lecture can do is to lead pupils vicariously through someone else's problem-solving experience, in the same way as a well written monograph does. There is a place on the other hand for the teacher's exposition in the secondary school if it is considered as another resource of information at the disposal of the pupils. There is no doubt that a teacher's spoken description can often be more effective, especially as a stimulus, than the written paragraphs of a textbook. But if the teacher's own description or explanation is to contribute to the pupils' personal learning, it should meet the following conditions:

1   Teacher-exposition should occur within the context of problems that the *pupils* are trying to solve.
2   Such exposition should not consist of a monologue, but should include frequent questioning of the class to ensure that the pupils themselves are trying to find the answers to the historical problems.
3   Such exposition should not be the sole or even the major resource offered to pupils, and it should not be the main activity in any one lesson.

It is useful for the teacher to introduce a problem or set the scene for the investigation of an historical event. He may need to provide a connection between a new topic or concept and those previously studied. Some teachers have a talent for bringing historical events to life and may therefore want to regale a class with exciting descriptions of historical events or characters or the narration of spicy historical incidents. But no matter how gifted a teacher is in that line, his gifts should never become the major resource for learning simply because the description or narration supposes that for most of the learning experience pupils are required to remain physically and mentally passive. Pupils cannot learn historical thinking by listening to the thoughts of somebody else. They must be allowed to do it for themselves.

Models of History Teaching

Telling a story

The one type of historical exposition which is suitable for the school classroom is the direct narration of a particular historical story. A well told story can be of great value in exciting the imaginations of young people provided that the intrinsic interest of the event described is matched by a convincing performance from the story-teller. Many ten- or fifteen-minute stories about people can be found in political or military history. Biographical illustrations can be also used in social or economic history. But if a story is intended to provide a source for information about social or economic structures, then it is better to allow the pupils to read the printed word for themselves and make them analyse what they read by careful questioning. Spoken stories are therefore not suitable for every learning objective, nor for every type of history studied in a secondary school. They should never become the dominant method in any individual teacher's instructional style. Even where the story-teller is exceptionally talented, too great a reliance on that sort of exposition would restrict pupils to a narrow range of historical experience and limit its contribution to their general intellectual development.

The born story-teller does, however, have an advantage over ordinary mortals in the secondary school history classroom. By a choice of vocabulary that is both rich and precise, by intelligent modulation of the voice, and often by some physical expression of the drama being conveyed, he or she can bring an episode to life in a way that convinces children and adults alike. Most student teachers, on the other hand, even if they possess such qualities in embryo, have little confidence in their own powers until their ability has been confirmed by experience. Confidence results only from careful and sensible preparation of the story to be told.

Interest
Stories should not be regarded merely as time-fillers. They should play a specific part in an instructional sequence. If this part relates to creating interest or exciting the imaginations of pupils, the teacher should attempt to tell a dramatic story only if he is really gripped by it himself. And since the teacher's imagination may be caught by

incidents only peripherally related to the main narrative, he might
wish to tell a story which does not have any direct bearing on the
topic being studied. But where the objective is to arouse interest,
the peripheral nature of the subject matter should not deter the
teacher. Historical data central to the syllabus can be obtained from
other sources and be taught by other methods.

Detail

The intrinsic interest of an historical story lies usually in its detail
rather than in its relation to a larger narrative or argument. The
teacher should therefore research his matter thoroughly, using
biographies, memoirs, eye-witness accounts, and other sources to
augment the textbook, and by a detailed knowledge of the event
acquire the 'feel' as well as the 'facts'. Although he should never
attempt to replace factual detail by unbridled fancy a good knowledge
of historical background may occasionally enable the teacher to
make an intelligent guess at how some elements of his story should
be imagined or described.

Timing

The effect of a story in the classroom can be improved if the timing
is right. This does not mean the speed of narration but rather the
time when the story is told. A story may of course be used at various
points in a teaching unit. It may introduce a topic in order to arouse
interest or it may enrich matter which has already been studied,
capitalizing perhaps on some interest already established. Hints
dropped by the teacher in anticipation of the story can, like the
'trailer' of a feature film, create a favourable atmosphere of expectation. 'There's an interesting story behind that incident, but we
haven't got time for it now. Perhaps next period.' The receptivity
of a class to story telling can be gauged from such a remark and
help the teacher to decide whether it is worth spending time on the
story or not.

　　In the actual performance of telling a story the teacher will have
to develop his own narrative talents. It is essential that the narration
does not dull the interest of the listeners. It should be well paced
and there should be enough variety of expression to give meaning

to the spoken words. Where a teacher has great confidence in his own ability or is very enthusiastic about the story itself, he must be sure at all times to keep in touch with his class. It is a mistake to be carried away into an excess of histrionics regardless of the reactions of the listeners.

An historical event needs to be described in simple concrete terms and without unnecessary elaboration. Abstractions and generalizations are usually unnecessary, and long introductions or distracting digressions should be avoided. The sooner listeners are involved in the heart of the matter the better. A young teacher uncertain of his own ability to tell a story well enough may occasionally fall back on the written word and read a passage from a popular historical author. This enables him to practise vocal dramatization and, if the author is really good, it might give him an insight into how a story should be structured. But the capacity to describe historical episodes in original words, words which appeal to a certain class or age group and develop their understanding and imagination, can only come from the teacher's own efforts and experience.

A designer of learning

If the school history teacher is not supposed simply to explain history to his pupils in the way that the university or college lecturer does, what then is his function? It would be wrong to suppose that a problem-solving approach to history teaching creates a less important role for the teacher. On the contrary, the teacher's tasks are not diminished but enlarged. He is no longer concerned simply with knowledge: soaking up the contents of the textbooks and works of reference and then spilling it out to his listeners. He is concerned with thinking and its development, and to that end he becomes a designer of the sort of learning experience through which his pupils will acquire the historical dimension of their personal *gestalt*.

Part of a teacher's function has often been repeated in the types of history lesson described earlier. The teacher has to present the problem, to show pupils to what ends they are required to think and then to help them by the way he conducts his lessons to think their way through to those ends. Another part of his duties lies in the organization of aids and resources. The distinction between these two concepts is an important one for the way in which history is going to be taught. Any given map, chart, picture, etc. can be used as an aid if it serves to clarify, illustrate, or reinforce a concept or render it more concrete. But such items can also be used as resources from which the pupils draw their information, or the evidence from which a narrative has to be constructed. A reproduction of a handbill advertising a slave auction in Jeffersonian Virginia may be used as an illustration of one aspect of slavery, with the object of interesting the class or making the slave system seem more real. But that handbill can also be used as a resource from which the pupils are required to infer certain information about slavery and its manner of operation.

Publishing companies whose main target is the educational market have made all teachers aware of the vast quantity and variety of educational materials now available for use in the classroom. The advertising may make some teachers feel guilty if they have not equipped a specialist history room with all kinds of beautiful maps and three-dimensional models. But the importance of educational materials lies not in their beauty but in their use. And if the approach to teaching is a problem-solving one, the emphasis is on using such materials as resources for the pupils' own activities. Visual aids are certainly important, but they are secondary.

Planning instruction

In the practical world of secondary school teaching, learning experiences are normally organized according to specific patterns: syllabuses divide into years, years divide into terms, terms divide into units of study, and the units themselves are divided into single lessons. The largest organizational unit with which most beginners are concerned is the year's work. The problems of syllabus construction for a year or longer will be considered in the final chapter of this book. But here we are concerned with a teacher's duties in organizing the term's work and planning individual lessons.

It is very easy for the inexperienced teacher to fall into the 'syllabus trap'. Faced with the task of planning the work of thirteen weeks with a large number of pupils whose intellectual capabilities are unknown, many teachers fall back on the printed syllabus and follow it topic by topic in the hope that it will be successfully completed by the end of the term. If a teacher relies mainly on information study, then he will probably get through the syllabus, but the educational value of that breathless gallop will be minimal. If on the other hand a teacher tries to persuade his pupils to think about the issues raised by the topics studied without careful planning, he will find that he does not get through the syllabus at all.

A teacher who has a proper concern for the intellectual development of his pupils needs to define clearly his educational goals, not simply which facts are to be learned but which thinking and study skills he has to impart as well. Once this is established, he can begin to plan in a systematic fashion. He should decide in which order the skills should be introduced, and with which topics certain skills ought to be exercised. He should study the syllabus and determine what approach to the historical content is called for, whether the study should emphasize patches or a line of development or a combination of several of the classic systems. The proximity of an external examination has to be considered and the influence of other subjects on the historical content or skill requirement need to be examined.

The teacher should then try to fit all his objectives into the time allotted to the course. He will probably find that some pruning needs to be done if he is to cover the essentials satisfactorily by the end of the term. There is always a temptation to sacrifice time-consuming skill exercises to greater content coverage, and the solution to that dilemma depends how much the teacher relies on pupils knowing historical 'facts' and how much on their ability to make use of them. With the course subdivided into units of study, each with a strict time allotment, the teacher can turn to the question of teaching methods, resources, and assessment.

Planning lessons

The planning of a single lesson requires the same systematic approach as has been suggested for a term's teaching. An effective lesson is usually one which has been carefully thought out and executed as a balance of many different forces. The individual lesson is of course only one step in a much larger sequence of learning. But the larger sequence depends for its effectiveness on all the links in the chain of instruction, all the individual lessons. Thus the first consideration of the teacher is to see that each lesson makes a contribution to a progressive learning sequence, as well as constituting a separate unit of instruction of its own. Many other factors influence the planning of a lesson, including the pupils themselves and their normal response to teaching of different sorts, the time of day and week, and the demands of the content and availability of resources.

Given such considerations the teacher should plan according to a basic system: the designation of objectives must come first, then a decision about methods of instruction, and finally an evaluation of how much the pupils have learned. Many colleges or departments of education produce a 'lesson plan form' which they insist their students use for teaching practice lessons or college assignments. There are many different kinds of lesson plan, most of them equally valid. It does not really matter what format is used as long as it includes all the essential elements and as long as some systematic form of planning is undertaken. You have already seen three examples of lesson plans reproduced earlier in Figures 3, 5, and 6 (see pp. 24, 36, and 66).

Most lesson plans will include the following information:
objectives;
content notes;
resources and aids;
methods and pupil activities;
follow-up and assignments.

Objectives
Even if the objectives do not appear at the top of a lesson plan, they must come first in any thinking about the lesson. Objectives need not be constructed in as rigid terms as those described by Robert Mager (see 'Further reading' section), but they should satisfy two important conditions:

a) Objectives should be written in terms of the pupil; they should describe what the *pupil* is going to do during the lesson, not what the teacher is going to do. Thus the statement that the teacher will teach about the Klondike Gold Rush is not an acceptable objective. It is a description of the teacher's activity rather than the objective or purpose of that activity.

b) Objectives should refer both to *content* and *skill* coverage in the lesson, and should therefore describe what pupil activity is to be applied to a certain content. So a teacher might state as one of his objectives: 'The pupils should be able to imagine the conditions experienced by the gold seekers travelling the Klondike trail' or 'The pupils should be able to describe in a short paragraph how the Klondike Gold Rush led to the opening of the Yukon to European exploitation.'

Content notes

Every teacher, no matter how experienced, should make careful notes of the topic to be studied, especially when teaching a particular section of a syllabus for the first time. There are two main reasons for doing this:

a) The teacher must know the content himself. He would have to know it if he were going to lecture about it. But his knowledge needs to be deeper and more thorough if he is going to organize the learning activities of his pupils around the essential issues and themes, and if he is going to pick out the basic problems and lead his pupils towards solving them.

b) The teacher must be able to make a decision about what facts and insights he wants his pupils to gain from the study of the topic. Since teaching time is limited and history virtually limitless, this will in practice often mean deciding on the minimum that must be learnt without losing the value of teaching that topic.

In preparing for a unit of study a teacher should read not only the pupil's textbooks, but also many other secondary materials, and whatever primary sources are available to him. But when he comes to writing a lesson plan he should include only that information which he wishes his pupils to gain from the lesson. And he should organize his teaching notes in a logical way which suggests the ideas or themes through which the information is to be approached. Some teachers prefer not to include these on a lesson plan, but write them in a separate notebook. It does not matter where they are written as long as they are written somewhere, for it is often in the act of writing that a teacher clarifies his ideas about his real objectives in teaching a certain topic.

Resources and aids

Resources and aids should be prepared well before the lesson, but it is useful to note down any details on the lesson plan. This may be a help to the teacher who wants to check that he has everything for a lesson before he leaves the staffroom to go to the class. It will also act as a reminder when the teacher comes to repeat that lesson, perhaps as much as a year later. To this end the greater the detail noted, the easier it will be to find the materials again.

Methods or pupil activities

This should be the core of any lesson plan just as it is the centre of any lesson. How are the pupils going to learn? There are many considerations which may influence the teacher's choice of activities for a particular lesson, but it is important that the following principles be observed:

a) There should be a variety of activities during a forty-minute lesson. In most of the models described earlier more than one type of activity was mentioned. Secondary school pupils should not normally be expected to do the same thing (read, listen, discuss) for nearly an hour: if they do their capacity for learning will gradually disappear as the lesson wears on. Mental activity and energy are essential for effective learning, and for the young such energy usually depends on sustained interest. In some situations, such as a double period of model-making or project work, interest may be maintained over a long exercise, but these exercises have an inbuilt variety that the reading of a textbook does not have. Whether all the different activities of the lesson apply to the same resource or are directed to various resources, there must be enough variety to prevent boredom—the greatest enemy of learning.

b) At least one of the activities of any lesson should involve the pupils working either individually or in groups. No lesson should be monopolized by the teacher. At some stage the pupils must be given the opportunity to take an active part in a lesson as well as to look or listen.

c) The planned activities must follow from the established objectives of the lesson. Thus if one of the objectives is that the pupils should be able to write, then they must be permitted to spend part of the lesson time in writing.

Having decided on the main activities to be introduced in order to achieve the set objectives, the teacher then needs to work out how to arrange the activities and how to organize the lesson. In making organizational decisions the teacher should be guided both by the nature of the problem to be presented and the resource upon which it depends, and by the needs and habits of the pupils. Some classes like to tackle difficult work on their own while others need very careful guidance for anything which is not extremely simple. In some places group work has become a fashion and has been overworked, to the detriment of individual learning. Group discussion is useful when there is a problem or controversial issue which may be solved by a combined effort, and also of course in simulation or project work which requires more than one pupil to be done effectively. A teacher may also ask a class to work in small groups when he feels that the atmosphere in a classroom could be improved by a change: this is especially useful in a small class. But it must always be remembered that in the final analysis we are trying to teach the *individual child*, and it is important that no child misses out on a learning experience. There is a danger in the modern classroom of using too much group work and too much full class discussion and insufficient individual work. The teacher should bear this in mind when planning lesson activities.

Many lesson plans show separate spaces for indicating beginnings and endings of lessons. Much has been written by educationists on how lessons should start, with the stress on 'mind capture'. It is hardly necessary to add to that literature here. It is obviously desirable to interest pupils at the beginning of a lesson—and all the way through it—but it is fatal to spend so much effort making an exciting beginning that the real focus of the lesson is missed. Usually the faster one gets into the main activities of the lesson and the briefer the introduction the better. It is also unnecessary to preface every new lesson with a recapitulation of what has been learned in the previous lesson. This can act as the reverse of mind capture, and can be a deterrent to pupils who are waiting to be interested by something new and find themselves rehearsing what they already know.

As for endings, most teachers are mainly concerned about ending lessons on time. It is possible to set a homework assignment before the end of the forty-minute period and let pupils start on it in lesson time. This has the advantage of flexibility and gives the teacher a chance to see that the pupils have understood the assignment and will not waste homework time by doing something that has not been asked for. In general, beginnings and endings of lessons should have variety rather than conform to a never-changing routine. Variety is not necessarily the only spice of life but it does help to prevent boredom.

Follow-up and assignments
Homework assignments should either reinforce the skills and knowledge the pupils have acquired from a lesson or series of lessons, or carry those skills and knowledge forward into new areas of experience. Homework can provide a link between lessons or units of instruction. It can also provide a means of assessing whether and to what extent instructional objectives have been achieved. It is very important in a subject like history that the teacher keeps track of the development of his pupils. It is easier in history to let pupils go from lesson to lesson without really establishing whether they have learnt anything than it is in, say, a foreign language or mathematics. Both classroom and homework assignments can be used to evaluate pupils' progress long before normal examinations have to be set. The following chapter deals in greater detail with the evaluation of learning and its place in education. But it is something which must be considered while lessons are being planned. But to prevent follow-up assignments becoming a subsidiary form of testing for knowledge, teachers should make considerable use of homework as a means of practising and improving skills.

Marking homework assignments is of course a great problem for the overburdened teacher. Little is more conducive to despair than the piles of exercise books which often face a teacher at home after he has finished his supper. On the other hand, if homework is begun during classtime then the lesson itself must be curtailed. The answer lies in being realistic: in not overburdening the pupils with long assignments and not overburdening oneself with an impossible problem of marking. The importance of marking is that it should be an aid to learning: it should help pupils to improve their skills. It is therefore doubly necessary that it be done carefully and methodically rather than quickly and in vast quantities.

All these separate elements form a part of the process of planning a lesson. To the experienced teacher they are a routine operation, and many teachers would be surprised if it were pointed out what they were doing, so much do they become part of a teacher's working life. The perfect lesson is one which achieves perfect integration of all the competing needs of syllabus, community, and pupil, and most teachers would agree that it is a rare phenomenon. But teaching is an art, and in that respect it is like the *gestalt* that we form in our minds: the whole is greater than the parts of which it is composed. Each teacher will develop an individual style, and this style will be adapted to suit various categories of pupils, but when analysed all successful teaching contains much the same elements.

Exercises

1 Write a set of objectives for a lesson that you are planning, considering both skills and content. Begin each objective with the phrase 'The pupils should be able . . .'
2 Draw up a complete lesson plan including content notes for a senior form on any topic you choose. Indicate after each activity the amount of time you have allowed.
3 Draw up a series of three of four lesson plans on a single topic to be taught to a first-year class. The plans should include a variety of resources.

Further reading

W.J. Popham and Eva L. Baker, *Establishing instructional goals,* Prentice-Hall (New Jersey, 1970).

W.J. Popham and Eva L. Baker, *Planning an instructional sequence,* Prentice-Hall (New Jersey, 1970).

W.J. Popham and Eva L. Baker, *Systematic instruction,* Prentice-Hall (New Jersey, 1970).

Robert Mager, *Preparing instructional objectives,* Fearon Publishers (Palo Alto, 1962).

Norman E. Gronlund, *Stating behavioural objectives for classroom instruction,* Prentice-Hall (New Jersey, 1969).

Tom Hastie, *History after four o'clock,* The Historical Association (London, 1971).

Norman W. Beswick, *School Resource Centres,* Schools Council Working Paper 43. Evans/Methuen Educational (London, 1972).

Part 2
Assessment in history

11

Assessment as the evaluation of history learning

There is a well established tradition in secondary schools that, once it has been taught, history has to be examined. Sometimes it is examined internally by the teachers who have been responsible for the instruction. Sometimes it is examined externally by boards of examiners who sit in judgement on the efforts of both pupils and teachers. The whole problem of examinations, particularly external ones, is vexed and their influence on history as it is taught in schools will be studied in the next chapter. But before examining the commonest current procedures for testing historical knowledge, we intend to take a look at the principles not only behind formal examinations but behind all types of assessment of student learning. We will try to define the main problems and to suggest possible solutions to two basic questions: Why should we assess history, and if we assess it, what forms should that assessment take?

Purposes of assessment

Firstly, the teacher of history should be aware that 'assessment' does not necessarily mean 'examinations'. All forms of evaluating what the pupils have been learning, which will be categorized below, are considered here under the umbrella term 'assessment'. And assessment as an act of evaluation is something which continues one way or another throughout the pupil's learning and the teacher's instruction. It is an integral part of the learning process. Secondly, any student of education should know that the empirical study of assessment has become a sub-discipline within the area of professional education studies. Some of the basic textbooks in that sub-discipline are listed in the 'Further reading' section at the end of this chapter and will be referred to during the following paragraphs. But it is important for the history teacher to realize that the purposes and problems in assessing pupil or student learning are not necessarily peculiar to the discipline of history: many other subjects taught at almost any level of education or training involve similar issues.

The basic purpose of assessment is integral to teaching or instruction itself. If we define teaching as 'helping pupils to learn', it becomes evident that a continuous exercise in teaching, or a succession of teaching units, will achieve the desired objective only if the teacher knows that the early parts of the exercise have been successfully learned. Classroom teaching is aimed either at changing some of the ways in which pupils act—the ways they think, write or argue—or at offering pupils an opportunity to develop individual potentialities which enable them to change their own behaviour. Such changes can only be effected through a sequence of instruction, and an essential pre-requisite of progressing to a new stage within that sequence is the successful mastery of an earlier stage. Now it is at this point in the discussion of assessment that many history teachers opt out. History is not a sequenced discipline like French language or mathematics. One can successfully tackle the nineteenth century in the fifth year of a secondary school without having ploughed through the eighteenth century in the fourth year. This lack of content sequence leads teachers to assume that a sequenced assessment of pupil learning is of little importance in history and that the main purposes of testing are the provision of 'marks' for the compilation of a class aggregate and as a means of ranking pupils, or the preparation of pupils for the serious hurdles of public examinations.

But there is a sequence in the learning of history, and this sequence is to be found not within the topics studied but in the historical skills developed. In practice of course one teaches historical skills through the history narrative, just as one masters the narrative by means of and in conjunction with the necessary skills. But the lack of a necessary sequence in the content should not blind us to the existence of a developmental sequence of skills. In this respect it is more than useful that the performance of pupils in exercising historical skills should be assessed from time to time. If it is left to the 'Certificate year' many pupils will do less well than they should because there is no time to retrace steps and establish basic abilities which should have been mastered a year or two earlier.

If the main purpose of evaluation in history learning is to establish to what extent a pupil has mastered the skills integral to the acquisition of historical knowledge, then it is obvious that before any form of evaluation is designed or chosen, the skills (as well as the content) to be evaluated must be clearly specified. This means two things: the objectives of the assessment must relate to the results expected of a certain course of study; and the form the assessment takes must correspond to the objective for which the assessment is given. Moreover, any exercise in evaluating what pupils have learned in the past week or weeks presumably forms part of a series of assessment processes by which a teacher keeps track of the continuous progress of his pupils. The grades of one month's assignments are compared to those of the previous month, and the classroom test marks are recorded to show how individual pupils are improving or failing to improve as the course progresses. Thus, the success of any one assessment exercise depends on its place within a series and on whether the whole series is successfully related to the objectives of the course being taught and evaluated. As Norman E. Gronlund puts it in a standard textbook on the evaluation of learning (see 'Further reading' section), assessment is: 'a systematic process of determining the extent to which educational objectives are achieved' which involves 'two basic steps: (1) identifying and defining the objectives of instruction, and (2) constructing or selecting evaluation instruments which best appraise those objectives'.

Functions of assessment

While all assessment procedures have as their main purpose the measurement of pupil achievement in terms of the objectives of the course of study being followed, there are various reasons why pupil achievement needs to be measured. We call these 'functions' rather than purposes of assessment, but it is important that a teacher is aware of the function of assessment, since the type of evaluation he uses can be affected as much by the function as it is by the specific course objectives. The principal divisions of function in assessment are as follows:

Formative function

This is to help the pupil improve his current learning. An assignment given to a pupil to establish whether he has mastered a specific skill is an example of formative assessment, since it indicates either that the pupil is ready for instruction in new skills or topics, or that he needs remedial work or reinforcement to help him succeed with the unit of instruction he is at present following. Thus a pupil who fails miserably in an assignment or test in map interpretation will need special work set for him if he is to keep up with the rest of the class in a topic which calls for considerable map-work.

Formative diagnosis

This is a diagnostic function which relates to exercises given not only to see whether a pupil has mastered a skill, but to establish how he has mastered it or how he has failed to do so. Before setting additional work for a pupil who cannot interpret maps, his problem has to be diagnosed rather more specifically. Is his problem an inability to read simple cartographic symbols? Does he fail in transferring symbolic knowledge (out of a written text) to a graphic form or back again? Or is he simply ignorant of basic principles of geography? Extra work will not help unless it is the right kind of work, structured to help him overcome the failings that have been diagnosed.

Summative function

At the end of a course a decision has usually to be made whether and to what extent a pupil has achieved the sum of the course objectives. Here the purpose is not to assist current learning but to evaluate the effectiveness of past learning. The result of a summative assessment may of course determine what type of future course will be useful or possible. It may also be related to matters outside the course sequence, e.g. whether a pupil will take 'O' levels, or whether he will go on to tertiary education.

147

Summative diagnosis
If the object of the summative evaluation is to determine the pattern of future studies, then it will be helpful to determine not only whether a pupil has 'passed' or not, but where he is strong in that subject area and where he is weak. A pupil may have a good head for historical facts and pass excellently at objective tests, but may be weak in writing and poor at historical interpretation. Such a diagnosis may help to decide what type of study will be of real assistance to the pupil in the next session, not only in terms of the discipline of history but in terms of the pupil's general intellectual development.

This categorization of assessment by its basic function within the educational sequence of the pupils is not a purely academic exercise even for the history teacher. The type of assessment should obviously reflect its general function, and while public examinations are obviously summative in function, term assignments and short tests in class are usually formative. But in that case is an old GCE question suitable for a formative assignment? The answer is: not unless the objective of the exercise is to give pupils practice in the testing procedures of the GCE. The formative function of ordinary assignments demands that the teacher design a question which helps a pupil either to exercise the knowledge and skills he has just acquired or establishes whether he is having difficulty with that part of the course. The GCE question will rarely do that.

Varieties of assessment

When authors use the term 'evaluation instruments' they are referring to the methods by which evaluation or assessment can be made in teaching. Evaluation is a larger concept than simply the types of test which can be given. For assessment is not merely testing, it is a form of judgement which can be made by a variety of methods, and each of these methods has a specific use for the evaluation of certain types of learning.

Intuitive or estimated assessment
This is the type of assessment which Martin Booth describes (see 'Further reading' section) as:

the broad unspecified assessment of the pupil's progress and development with which the able teacher is constantly concerned and which forms the hallmark of any valid teaching situation.

A good teacher is intuitively in touch with his class. In many cases he can estimate whether the pupils are progressing simply by his interpretation of normal classroom interaction. For certain aspects of history teaching there is no other way to find out whether pupils are reaching the desired objectives. This is true for those results of history teaching which are unquantifiable, but which should not therefore be considered impossible to assess. A history teacher should awaken a spark of genuine historical interest in his pupils. He will know whether he has succeeded in this by the random remark, the style of classroom response, the general manner of a child engaged in the study of history, rather than by any written test. A question-naire, for example, is of very doubtful value, although it may as a diagnostic exercise help a teacher to see why some of his pupils are *not* interested in his lessons. The sort of data which the teacher uses in forming his intuitive or estimated evaluation cannot really be classified. It is what Gronlund terms 'anecdotal information'. Nor is it always possible to record it, except in rare cases, for example, with a child whose difficulties make a minute record of his class-room behaviour a valuable teaching instrument. But the intuition of the practitioner is a form of assessment, and in evaluating the whole of a pupil's record that assessment should also be taken into account, in so far as it relates to the specified objectives of the course the pupil has been following.

Structured assessment

Most accepted assessment procedures are purposely designed and administered in order to enable a teacher at a specific time to evaluate some aspect of pupil learning. But again, structured assessment does not only mean examinations. It can be divided into two types.

Continuous assessment   This is a systematic evaluation of the pupil's work done over a specified period or course. To be valid, such assessment must cover all the major objectives of the course.

And since the teacher's memory is fallible, it is better to keep a record of each pupil. Here the representative nature of the teacher's record is important. One-word-answer tests on factual information are easy to score. Time-lines are difficult. If a teacher therefore records only the factual tests and does not record grades for the time-line assignments, his record will be defective for a course which has as its object the development of skills in chronology. Of course, the use of a problem-solving approach in one's teaching, such as has been described in Part 1 of this book, makes the assessment of a course a good deal easier and helps to guarantee that the evaluation really does relate to the objectives specified by the teacher.

Terminal assessment   This does not necessarily mean the examination given at the end of a school term, but rather the assessment organized at the termination of one course of instruction. This type of testing is formal in nature. The pupils know that a test is coming and will be administered in a way which prevents them from being helped by their friends. It is accepted by all concerned that the results of such assessment carry a certain weight in the evaluation of a pupil's over-all record. Here it is important to remember that precisely because of its formal nature, too much terminal testing can ruin a course, kill interest, and arouse pupils' hostility. Moreover, the use of terminal testing procedures in continuous assessment, weekly exams, written or oral, on textbook knowledge, can distort the nature of a course, obliging the pupils to concentrate their attention on passing examinations rather than enjoying and learning from history. Terminal testing can be formative or summative in function. It should not have as its main object the awarding of marks—an '82' for history to be computed against a '65' for English to provide an aggregate which has no educational relevance to either course. This is a misuse of assessment procedures which is encouraged by the practice of turning course evaluation into marks out of a hundred. A grade at the end of a year's work is a reasonable request, however, and it is much more useful to know that a child was fair at history, good at mathematics, and poor at French than that he obtained 52% in history/mathematics/French. Again, the purpose and function of the assessment is important. If terminal assessment procedures, and the administration of them by headteachers or principals, bore some relation to the educational needs of the pupils then there would be no fear that the evaluation techniques used by a teacher might be misused or even distorted in the over-all grading of any individual child.

Criteria for assessment procedures

It is important for a teacher to be able to judge whether the assessment procedure he has designed and administered is a good one or not. Perhaps he may need to abandon a particular way of examining if it proves to be invalid. Or perhaps he can extend a particular method to other similar objectives within his course. Textbooks on assessment give a wide variety of criteria for deciding whether a test is suitable or otherwise. Here we mention only those which are both useful and practicable for the history teacher, who has neither the instruments at hand nor the time to compute the ratios and correlations with which a professional examiner or designer of standardized tests must be concerned.

Validity
It has already been mentioned that continuous assessment is only valid if it measures progress in all the major objectives of a particular course of study. A mark derived solely from factual tests is invalid as an evaluation of a complex course. So validity is established when the type of assessment really relates to the objectives of the course, and when the type of question in a test or assignment really relates to the objective of that assessment procedure.

If a test, for example, is intended to determine to what extent the pupils have successfully acquired a body of knowledge or a set of skills, then the content of the test must be valid. The questions in the test should examine abilities right across the content area and specified skills, rather than concentrate on a random selection of them. The history teacher is normally concerned with this sort of assessment when he is designing his annual examination. Other forms of assessment which involve comparing results in one test to achievement in other subjects or forms of evaluation are important for classroom teachers only when they are involved in constructing public examinations.

Usability
This is of practical concern for the classroom teacher, and comprises several considerations which may often prove problematical to the inexperienced. Can the test be done? This may mean: Can it be done in the time set? Can the necessary resources be obtained for the candidates? For example, will the photocopying facilities available in the school satisfactorily reproduce the pictures a teacher might want to present for interpretation? Is it going to be too expensive? Can the test be marked easily? It is often true that the simpler types of question are the most difficult to mark; it is therefore useful to design the marking scheme at the same time as the question and sometimes to revise the question to bring it more into line with the only practicable scheme of marking it.

Reliability
Does the assessment give an accurate picture of the pupils' abilities and achievements both as seen in the results of one procedure and compared with the results of previous evaluation? If a teacher sets three tests during a year, and finds that there is absolutely no correlation between the results of any of them, then it is likely that there is something wrong with the testing. A test is also unreliable as an indication of pupil performance if all the candidates get marks within a very narrow range. If everybody gets a grade of 'good', in a test designed to assess one specific skill with a clear criterion then all the pupils may possibly have reached a high standard, and that grade may be acceptable. But if the evaluation is of a complex nature, the grading should be extended in order to discriminate between those who have mastered all and those who have mastered only some of the desired learning skills. Where there is no single clear criterion for establishing whether pupils have grasped a particular skill or not, the teacher must decide on a norm by which he can determine the ratings of pupils, even if the grading is as simple as 'good, bad and middling'.

What sort of assessment is suitable for history?

Since the form of assessment used in a particular situation is to be determined by the objectives to be evaluated, then the type of assessment chosen depends on what the individual teacher has set as the objectives of his course. For most teachers, certainly, these objectives, in the words of Martin Booth, 'go far beyond the mere accumulation of data' and include 'mental skills of understanding and evaluating and emotional responses of receiving and sympathizing'. Not all of these objectives can be assessed by written examination, and as has been mentioned above, the teacher has to rely on his own intuition in evaluating the responses of, for example, sympathy and interest. And since personal intuition is impossible to justify in any but the most subjective terms, this form of assessment is often not included in any permanent way in a pupil's record. But because it is not recorded it does not follow that such evaluation is unimportant. Assessment is not made for the record. Formative assessment in particular is meant to assist the learning process, and learning, like teaching, is an activity in which the subjective and the intuitive have roles to play. Assessment therefore is not invalidated because it derives from interaction between a pupil and his teacher. Such interaction is the stuff of much successful teaching.

If the 'artistic' response of a pupil to the subject of history can be assessed only in an unstructured intuitive way, the intellectual and imaginative skills as well as the factual knowledge acquired can be evaluated in assignments and tests. It is obviously better for purposes of assessment to evaluate different objectives by different exercises rather than to attempt to use one means of evaluation to cover all the desired learning objectives. This is the weakness as well as the strength of the traditional history essay. While it can be used to test a wide variety of objectives, factual knowledge, summarization, categorization, skills of criticizing, synthesizing, imagining, etc., a practical marking scheme can only be devised to assess two or three of those objectives. And all too often it is the easily assessed factual knowledge which is evaluated in a 'good essay' rather than other more problematic though no less important objectives. It is better for the teacher to separate the achievements he wants to measure and allot to each a suitable testing procedure: *objective testing* for factual knowledge and simple cognitive skills, *interpretative testing* for powers of comprehension and critical interpretation, and *essay-type testing* for the abilities involved in assembling evidence, arguing a case, and synthesizing knowledge.

A teacher who wishes to conduct a successful exercise in assessment must organize it in a systematic way. This involves adhering to a few straightforward principles of evaluation design:

1 Take into consideration the general function of the assessment (formative, summative, or diagnostic) and structure your tests or exercises to that general aim.
2 Specify which instructional or learning objectives you want the assessment to measure.
3 Construct each question or exercise so that the correct pupil response can only be given by exercising the required skill or producing the required knowledge.
4 Ensure that each question or exercise is appropriate to the comprehension level of the class and the level of understanding proper to the course given.
5 Before finalizing the assessment, check that the skills and knowledge called for are representative of the whole course which is meant to be evaluated.

In the light of these procedures, exercises can be given for continuous assessment, and tests can be set for examination purposes. Below we outline the various types of test question which are suitable for measuring learning in history.

Objective testing

Objective tests are those in which the candidate's response is limited to a single word or phrase or a simple choice from several solutions presented to him. Objective questions are best used for testing knowledge of precise information or ability in simple skills. In history they are commonly used for evaluating mastery of:

Specific facts;
Historical terms;
Historical periods;
Recognition of concepts;

Recognition of relationships;
Recognition of methods of research.

There are five principal types of objective test suitable for history assessment:

1 Short answer tests

Example   *a*) In what year did India achieve its independence?
             b) What is the name of the wind which blows periodically across the Indian Ocean?

2 Short completion tests

Example   *a*) India achieved its independence in the year ....
             b) The wind which blows periodically across the Indian Ocean is called the ....

These two types of objective test are simple to construct and to administer. They are suitable for less formal testing exercises in the classroom since the teacher can read the questions or write them on the chalkboard if he does not want the complications of cyclostyling the test and keeping it safe. They are useful for assessing knowledge of terminology or simple facts, and this is their limitation, for the sort of fact tested by a one-word answer is almost always trivial. And too much concentration on the trivia of historical knowledge is not going to help much in the development of general historical ability.

It is important to avoid short-cutting in these tests by means of putting several blank spaces in a one-word completion question.

Example Poor: The leader of the .... Party which
                      worked for .... in India
                      and who was assassinated in ....
                      was ....
      Better: *a*) The largest nationalist party in India before 1947 was called ....
              b) The acknowledged leader of the Indian independence movement was ....

3 Alternative response questions

Example   Read the following statements. If the statement is true circle the 'T'. If the statement is false, circle the 'F':

a) T F The Stamp Act of 1764 was an issue which led
to disagreement between American colonists and the
British Government.

b) T F The main American objection to the Stamp Duty was
that it imposed on Americans a tax not imposed in
Britain.

c) T F The Stamp Act imposed a duty on all papers required
in official transactions.

d) T F The Stamp Duty had never been imposed in the
American colonies before 1764.

e) T F The Stamp Duty was a type of indirect tax which was
part of the general system of regulation of trade.

The facts examined in this exercise can be more complex than those
tested in a short answer or completion question. However, the
obvious limitation is that the pupil must choose between what is
true and what is false without having to think why. The great
advantage of this kind of test is that it can easily be marked.
However, for this type of question to be adequate each statement
should:

a) be unambiguous;

b) be concrete rather than general;

c) be serious rather than trivial;

d) have a fairly simple grammatical structure;

e) have not more than one idea;

f) be approximately the same length as the other statements in the
question.

4 Matching exercises

Example Each of the following statements has two parts, a cause
and a result. But as they have been matched below, the results have
been separated from their proper causes. In the column below
match the letter of each result with the number of the cause to which
it should be related.

Cause	1	2	3	4	5
Result					

Cause	Result
1 Because there were wars in Arabia and Persia	A Sailors could travel more easily across the Indian Ocean
2 Because many Arabs married Africans	B Arabs came to live in East Africa
3 Because they were helped by monsoon winds	C Merchants were able to live extravagantly
4 Because they wanted to buy ivory and gold	D The Swahili people developed
5 Because they became rich from trade	E Indians came to East Africa

One use of this type of exercise is that it examines the ability to see relationships between events (such as the important relationship of cause and effect) and between categories of statement (particulars and generalizations). Its limitation is again that it evaluates recognition rather than understanding or analysis. Like all objective tests it is easy to mark. For adequate testing of the desired objective it is important that the exercise should:

a) indicate the basis for matching the two parts of the divided statements;

b) make use only of homogeneous information in one item;

c) avoid grammatical clues to matching the parts.

The danger of guessing (in a long series of matching tests, for example) can be avoided if there is an unequal number of premises and responses in each item. One well known example of the matching exercise is the time-line, in which events are matched against dates or against periods. Such questions are useful in testing a pupil's understanding of the chronology of a topic, of the sequence of events in time, the periodization within the topic and the relation in time of single events either to a cluster of closely connected happenings or to the broad sweep of history. Time-lines therefore tend to examine rather different things if they are devoted to a restricted area or period (e.g. West African savanna kingdoms, A.D. 800-1000) or to a larger scope (European history from Caesar to Stalin). Again there are several different ways of constructing a time-line:

1   Candidates can be asked simply to place events in their proper chronological order;

2   Candidates can be asked to match events with a precise date on a printed time-line;

3   Candidates can be asked to place events within a period on a printed time-line.

The following examples show three different types of time-line test on Canadian history:

a) Arrange the following events in the history of the Canadian West in the order in which they occurred:
    (i)   The Manitoba Act
    (ii) The Riel Rebellion in the Red River Colony
    (iii) Canadian Government sends an armed force to the Saskatchewan River
    (iv) Canadian Pacific Railway completed
    (v)   Louis Riel hanged
    (vi) Alberta and Saskatchewan become provinces
    (vii) Outbreak of North-West Rebellion
    (viii) Second contract between Canadian Government and the Canadian Pacific for the building of the railway
    (ix) Disputes between European immigrants and Metis along the Saskatchewan River
    (x)   British North America Act
    (xi) Pacific Scandal

b) Place the events in the list below next to the correct date on the time-line. Write only on the lines provided.
    (i)   NATO alliance formed
    (ii) Winnipeg general strike
    (iii) Wilfrid Laurier forms his first government
    (iv) Responsible government in East and West Canada
    (v)   British North America Act
    (vi) Completion of the Canadian Pacific Railway
    (vii) Popular rebellions in Upper and Lower Canada
    (viii) Conscription Act
    (ix) New Democratic Party formed
    (x)   Statute of Westminster

Assessment as the evaluation of history learning

1835 _____

1845 _____

1855 _____

1865 _____

1875 _____

1885 _____

1895 _____

1905 _____

1915 _____

1925 _____

1935 _____

1945 _____

1955 _____

1965 _____

c) Each of the following events occurred during one of the twenty-five year periods indicated by the time-line. Put the letter of each event in the correct box.

A	Struggle between Hudson Bay Co. and Montreal traders for control of the North-West	1600	
		1625	
B	First European exploration of the prairies to the Rockies	1650	
C	Loyalist immigrants settle Upper Canada and the Maritime colonies	1675	
D	French give up claims to Hudson Bay, Acadia, and Newfoundland	1700	
E	First French settlement along the St. Lawrence	1725	
F	Build-up of a fur trade empire from Montreal to the Mississippi Valley	1750	
G	British colonies in North America unite under one federal government	1775	
H	New France conquered and ceded to Britain	1800	

159

I	Iroquois make several attempts to drive French settlers from Montreal, and fail	1825	
J	Establishment of a national economy based on a high tariff	1850	
K	Building of canals and railways in St. Lawrence—Great Lakes Valley	1875	
L	First missionary influx into New France	1900	

The marking of time-lines is sometimes thought to pose problems, and one author has even taken pains in a well known research test to work out the correlation coefficients for each of the answers in respect of the correct answer. Of course, if the question calls for the chronological ordering of a list of events and a certain candidate gets most of the order right but out of place (if for example he puts the seventh event where the first should be, but then gets events one to six in the correct order) a correlation coefficient would give him a properly high score. But so would any intelligently contrived marking scheme which weighted order more than position. And a time-line which requires the matching of events to dates or periods is even less of a problem to grade.

5   Multiple choice exercises
Example
a) In which of the following countries did the Industrial Revolution begin?
   (i) Germany
   (ii) United States of America
   (iii) Britain
   (iv) France
b) The Industrial Revolution began in:
   (i) Germany
   (ii) United States of America
   (iii) Britain
   (iv) France

A multiple choice question provides a question or an incomplete statement (the 'stem') and a number of possible responses or conclusions. The candidate's activity is limited to selecting the correct one out of the alternatives offered. Again this is a process of recognizing the right answer, but the form does permit the framing of complex statements or questions, for which the correct response can only be selected as a result of intelligent thought and knowledge of the processes of history. Thus multiple choice exercises are suitable for the recognition of:

historical facts and happenings;
principles or methods of inquiry;
relationships and concepts;
reasons and justifications;
conflicting interpretations.

Example Karl Popper maintained that because historical knowledge is always incomplete and an historian's view is necessarily partial then history can have no 'meaning'. From the following generalizations select that which Popper would therefore find unacceptable:

(i) All history is contemporary history
(ii) History has its uses
(iii) History reflects a view of society
(iv) History is progress.

There are two forms of multiple choice question, the question form and the incomplete statement form. And there are also two types of response which can be demanded, the *correct* response and the *best* response. While the best response type is suitable for questions which relate to principles ('Which of the following best illustrates the principle of . . .'), it is not a suitable form for exercises on historical facts or events. The best description of an event or the best explanation of a happening are likely to depend upon interpretation, and there is no reason why the candidate should always have the same interpretation as the examiner.

Example Avoid: Nineteenth-century imperialist penetration of Africa was caused by:

(i) Capitalist desire for cheap raw materials
(ii) Missionary evangelism and the struggle against the slave trade
(iii) The adventurous spirit of individual explorers and entrepreneurs
(iv) Rivalry for power between European nations
(Each of these alternatives may be understood to have contributed to the imperialist penetration of Africa. Which contributed most, or which alternative is the best, will always be a matter of opinion.)

To contruct a multiple choice exercise that provides a valid assessment, the teacher should observe the following guidelines:

a) All the questions in a multiple choice test should have the same number of alternative responses;

b) The correct response should not differ in length or general grammatical structure from the 'distractors';

c) All the alternatives should be grammatically consistent with the stem;

d) There should be only one correct answer among the alternatives;

e) All the alternatives should be plausible;

f) There should be no give-away verbal connection between the stem and the correct response;

g) The stem should contain the bulk of the statement, and the alternatives be kept as short as possible;

h) There should be no discernable regularity in the positioning of the correct responses among the alternatives;

i) Negative statements should be used only when a positive statement would make no sense for that item.

If an examination is given with a large number of multiple choice questions, there may be a chance that candidates obtain a proportion of marks for correct responses by random guessing. If this is thought likely, all the scores for the test should be amended by the standard formula for 'correction of guessing':

$$\text{Score} = \text{number of right answers} - \frac{\text{number of wrong answers}}{(n-1)}$$

Where n = number of alternative responses to each item

Thus a candidate who out of 100 items, each with four alternatives, got 64 right and 36 wrong would be given a corrected score of 52% $(64 - \frac{36}{(4-1)})$. This procedure is not recommended for ordinary classroom testing, but is advisable where long formal examinations are given by multiple choice.

Interpretative exercises

Example

a) Read the following passage and complete the exercises which follow it:

162

How does it strike you?
The Constitutional Question

The Trades Union Council deny that they are challenging constitutional government or that there is a constitutional issue. Yet at last year's meeting of the Council a speaker declared that they must make the Trades Union Council the real Parliament for the country. Moreover by ordering men to leave their work without notice they have aided and abetted not only wholesale breaches of law but of trade agreements and rendered employees liable to actions for damages.

The Council claim to be engaged in an industrial dispute. Yet the most uncompromising supporters of the strike are Communists —avowed enemies of the Constitution—Socialists, and all the lawless and most sinister and revolutionary elements in the country.

The Council profess to be fighting in the interests of the workers —yet by the wanton exercise of tyrannical power they have deprived thousands of breadwinners—great numbers of whom are not trade unionists and others not concerned in the dispute—of their means of livelihood and thrown them on the Poor Law and unemployment exchanges.

(*Hackney Gazette*: Daily Emergency News Bulletin, 12 May, 1926)

   (i) Does the second sentence of the passage ('Yet at last year's . . .') effectively disprove the claim of the TUC that there was no constitutional issue in the 1926 strike? Give *one* reason for your opinion.
  (ii) Why do you think that the government supporters made the 'constitutional issue' a major part of their argument against the strike? Give *one* reason.
 (iii) Explain how the 1926 strike might have deprived non-trade-unionists of their livelihood. Give *one* way.
  (iv) Knowing that Hackney was a poor inner suburb in the East End of London, what local interests do you think the *Hackney Gazette* was representing? Give *three* suggestions.
   (v) What effect do you suppose the *Hackney Gazette* leader might have had on the workers supporting the strike in the East End of London? Write no more than *three* sentences.

 b) Read the following passage and complete the exercises that follow it:

Lord Balfour Answered

Day by day in the Cabinet newspaper Mr. Churchill, acting as its super-editor, publishes articles by prominent public men. They are suspiciously like one another. This morning's contribution is signed 'Balfour' but the hand almost all through is the hand of Churchill, who is trying, still, to create panic by representing an industrial dispute about wages as an attempted revolution. Lord Balfour knows perfectly well that the trade unions have no revolutionary, no political aims. They are simply doing their utmost in the only way open to them to prevent the wages of an important body of workers from being driven down to a point which the mine-owners themselves have admitted to be 'miserable'. The reference to the strike being directed by a 'relatively small body of extremists' again betrays Mr. Churchill's hand. It is mere violent, headlong, foolish propaganda—foolish because no sensible person will believe it. It is impossible that Lord Balfour can suppose Mr. Pugh, Mr. Thomas, Mr. Bevin and other members of the General Council, who have always been moderate reasonable men, to have been suddenly transformed into 'extremists' as rash and reckless as Mr. Churchill himself.

(i) Winston Churchill was at this time a member of the:
    A   Communist Party
    B   Independent Labour Party
    C   Fabian Society
    D   Conservative Party

(ii) The article signed by Lord Balfour maintained that:
    A   Britain was in the throes of revolution
    B   All the strikers were reckless extremists
    C   The strike was inspired by political ends
    D   Modest reasonable men should take over the TUC

(iii) The wages which were at the heart of the dispute were those of:
    A   Members of the General Council of the TUC
    B   Activists of the Hackney Communist Party
    C   Coal miners all over the country
    D   All trade unionists

(iv) The newspaper from which this leader is taken appears to have been the organ of:
    A   The British Communist Party
    B   The political wing of the strike committee
    C   The Labour Party
    D   The Trades Union Congress

(v) The writer of the leader intends that:
    A   British employers should stop supporting Mr. Churchill
    B   Leaders of the TUC be replaced
    C   Lord Balfour agree to discuss with the TUC
    D   Lord Balfour accept that the strike is industrial, not political

Interpretative exercises are based on historical material about which pupils have to answer questions. This material must be new to the pupils but should relate to an historical topic with which they are familiar. This device enables the assessor to control the amount of factual material upon which the pupil exercises his historical abilities. It is therefore especially valuable in assessing skills, including:

translation;
imaginative reconstruction from partial evidence;
drawing of inferences;
testing hypotheses.

In the examples given above, primary historical evidence has been used, but other material may also be used for such exercises:

secondary passages;
maps;
statistical data;
pictures;
charts and diagrams, etc.

An example of an interpretative map question is shown in Figure 11. In each case questions can be framed to test the pupils in the skills necessary for understanding the type of resource used in the exercise. If a secondary source is used, for example, the questions would relate to critical comprehension, application of principles and method, recognition of assumptions and inferences, and the judging of warranted or unwarranted generalizations, rather than 'interpretation' of the sort suitable for primary evidence.

In the two examples given above, primary passages have been used which relate to the same historical events. It will be noticed immediately that this gives rise to a third possible series of questions: those which ask for a comparison of the two sources and their contents. In fact, two passages were given to show the possibility of framing either multiple choice or open-ended questions upon a passage given for interpretation. As can be seen from the examples, the thinking required of the candidates can be more ambitious if open-ended (essay-type) questions are used. But to prevent the pupils writing essays or very long paragraphs in their answers, the length of work required has to be specified. Thus we ask for 'one reason' or 'not more than three sentences'.

One objection, from experts in assessment, to this type of evaluation procedure is that it probably assesses aptitude rather than achievement. In any evaluation of skill (rather than of knowledge) it is always difficult to estimate how much of the skill has derived from the pupil's native intelligence and how much from the successful teaching of a particular course. Nor is it necessary for a teacher to know that in individual cases. But he should be concerned that his test is assessing the skills which have been exercised during course work. If the above examples had been given to a class which had never had that sort of experience before, a teacher would know that he was evaluating general intelligence and powers of transfer of training rather than specific skills. But if the teacher has used the methods explained in the model above on 'Document study', he will be able to frame questions which ask for precisely those skills which the pupils have already practised.

There is a danger when material is given in an interpretative test (which though new to the pupils relates strongly to the content area of the history they have been studying) that the teacher will be tempted to ask questions which do not relate to the material at all. 'What was Churchill's position in the Cabinet of 1926?' could have been an alternative to question (i) in passage (b) above. But it would have asked for information not contained in the passage and quite unimportant for its understanding. If factual knowledge

Figure 11   Map interpretation test

On the opposite page is a map of Ashante Trade in the eighteenth century. Study it carefully and answer the questions which follow:

a) Name four different groups of people with whom the Ashante people were trading in the eighteenth century.
b) Name two European trading posts in the eighteenth century.
c) Between which two trading areas did the people of Ashante act as 'middle men'?
d) Name two other peoples who were also in a position, as seen on the map, to act as middle men.
e) How many days do you think it might take a trader to travel on foot from Kumasi to Bonduku? Explain how you work out your answer.
f) What trade goods do you think were being carried northwards from Kumasi to Hausaland? Mention at least three.
g) Which journey do you think would be more difficult for an eighteenth-century traveller—from Kumasi to Gao or from Kumasi to Elmina? Give reasons for your answer.
h) Can you suggest a reason why the Ashante wanted to expand their kingdom as far as the Atlantic coast?

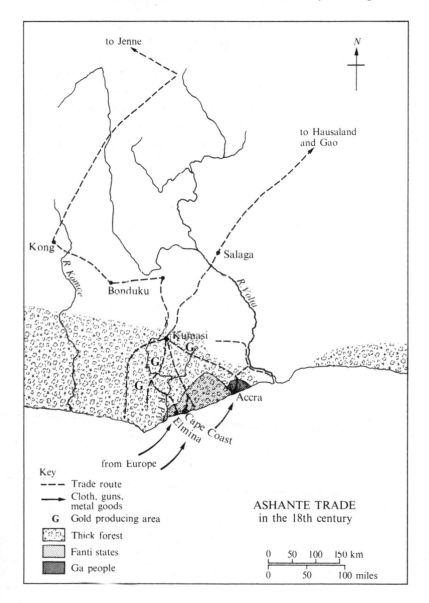

Figure 11   Map interpretation test

about the 1926 General Strike needs to be tested then objective tests should be designed to that end. To tack factual questions on to an interpretative exercise is poor assessment procedure, not least because it may encourage candidates to attempt to answer other questions from their memory in the same way as the factual questions.

In devising interpretative tests therefore the teacher should observe the following guidelines:

a) Material selected should be suitable for the objectives of the course being assessed.
b) Material selected should be new to the pupils, but at the level of their reading ability and general curricular experience.
c) The length of the introductory material should be commensurate with the number of questions asked: one question per sentence is perhaps ideal.
d) The introductory material should be as brief as possible within the bounds of comprehension and the objectives of the assessment.
e) All the questions should relate directly to interpretation, comprehension, or analysis of the material.

Essay-type questions

Essay-type or open-ended questions require that candidates solve given problems or provide narrative on a given topic in their own way, using their own knowledge and skills of organization and expression. There are two main forms of such questions:

Restricted-response questions
Example   We use the word 'revolution' to describe (i) the events of 1789-94 in France, (ii) the English industrial developments of the eighteenth and nineteenth centuries. What features *common* to both these periods allow one to describe them as 'revolutions'? Answer in not more than *two* sentences.
[From M.B. Booth, *History betrayed*, Longmans (London, 1969)]

Extended-response questions
Example
a) Give an account of the Cabal and its members and of their

counsels, and explain in what way they affected the state of England and of Europe.
[From University of London Matriculation Examination, November 1838]
b) Imagine that you are a member of John Churchill's staff in September 1688. Write a letter to a gentleman friend to persuade him to abandon his allegiance to James II and give his support to William and Mary.

One of the most important recent textbooks on assessment, the *Handbook of formative and summative evaluation of student learning* (see 'Further reading' section) admits that while objective tests 'do an excellent job in most cognitive areas', for those in which the student 'must create hypotheses of his own or draw conclusions without being provided with several conclusions from which to choose', the open-ended question must be used. In other words, history as a creative activity can only be evaluated by asking the pupil to create. To ask him to choose or recognize or to say 'yes' or 'no' is not enough. If the activity required of the pupil is simple (the analysis of the word 'revolution' and its application to two events) then a one-paragraph answer is sufficient. If a more complex activity of analysis, organization, and hypothesis is required, then the formal essay is suitable.

The two examples of the extended-response essay given above illustrate the two types of historical activity that can be assessed in that type of test:

a) An essay can assess the ability to present a coherent narrative, making use of and organizing evidence from a variety of sources, and showing powers of selection, logic, description, analysis of character, criticism, and analysis of conflicting opinions, etc.
b) An essay can assess the ability to use historical evidence in order to enter imaginatively into the past, either to construct a real picture of a happening or to create an imaginary happening within the historical context of the real.

The essay has been the traditional form of examining history for so long (at least since the 1838 Matriculation Examination quoted in an example above) that there is little need to justify it here. Instead we will consider three areas in which the essay as a form of assessment is vulnerable and suggest ways in which problems inherent to the form can be overcome.

How much should be assessed in a single essay?

The essay question is the best type of procedure for evaluating a pupil's ability to use his historical knowledge in a truly historical way. It is not the easiest or the best way to find out how much historical knowledge he has acquired. In practice, however, it not only proves difficult to distinguish between the amount of knowledge used and the way it is used; it is not easy to prevent assessment of the amount completely overshadowing evaluation of the manner of its use. So if a pupil is asked to write an essay on 'the causes of the First World War', the teacher is often tempted to specify mentally the number of 'causes' he wants the pupil to describe, and then give him a mark for each one. The way in which a pupil has successfully established that some occurrence was a cause, and the general organization of the essay, might be completely neglected in the assessor's marking scheme. Since it is supposed that a pupil's knowledge of the period will be assessed in a different sort of exercise, what is required is some way of ensuring that it is the *skill* of a pupil which is being credited in an essay, and not merely his knowledge.

There are two possible solutions to this problem:

a) A marking scheme can be devised which gives more credit to skill than to knowledge. The difficulty does remain however that without the knowledge the skill cannot be exercised. And a skilful pupil may be penalized for not knowing the content upon which he is supposed to exercise his skill. Many teachers would agree that this is the pupil's own fault, and that if the amount of knowledge is interfering with the use of knowledge in this case, it is only doing so in a negative way. The marking scheme does not give credit for knowing additional facts.

b) A guided essay can be set. That is to say, with the essay question the candidate can be presented with a set of notes, or headings of notes, as a memory aid. The skill assessed is the way in which a pupil uses these notes to construct a logical argument or convincing description.

Example To what extent did the Japanese seizure of Mukden in

Manchuria in 1931 contribute to the decline of civilian rule in Japan?
You may make use of the following considerations in your answer:
  (i) civilian and military composition of the cabinet in the Meiji
      constitution;
 (ii) military connections of the Seiyujaki and Minseito parties;
(iii) political effects of the assassination of Chang Tso-lin in
      1928;
 (iv) attack on Prime Minister Hamaguchi in 1930;
  (v) decline of the Genro as a power in politics;
 (vi) ministry of Inukei Tsuyoshi.

Formulation of an essay question
Because of the wide variety of assessment techniques for evaluating
factual knowledge and simple cognitive skills, it is better if essay
questions are limited to assessing objectives of a higher complexity
and cognitive order. In other words, it is better to use objective
tests for knowledge, interpretative tests for comprehension and
understanding, and essay tests for skills of synthesis and hypothesizing. And it is important that a teacher does not attempt to
assess too many of these higher-order skills in one essay. But just as
the teacher must know what he wants to assess, the candidate should
know equally clearly exactly what is expected of him. A question
like. 'Why was there a revolution in Russia in 1917?' may be asking
for several different things. The examiner may require a general
outline of Russian history from the beginning of the century to the
October Revolution. He may want a detailed study of the events of
1917: Why did the revolution occur in 1917 and not in 1916 or 1918?
Or he may want an analysis of Russian society and economy and
expect an explanation of its collapse: Why was a revolution
inevitable? It would obviously be much fairer for the pupils if the
examiner's wishes were made a little clearer:

Example   Describe the main political events in Russia between
1905 and 1917 and evaluate the various influences which brought
about revolution in that country by the end of 1917.

The key words here are 'describe' and 'evaluate'. The more concrete
the activity denoted by the introductory word the clearer the
instruction for the student. One wonders what pupils made of the
rubric of one public examination question which said: 'Write about
space exploration'. This sort of vagueness is suitable perhaps for an

171

English language essay, where the pupil can choose what to write about. But history is concerned with evidence and occurrences, and the candidate has a right to know exactly what he is expected to do with them.

In a classroom test it is true that pupils will often know what a teacher wants them to write even when it is badly expressed. In answering the question 'Why was there a revolution in Russia in 1917', pupils may be invited to repeat what their teacher has told them, which limits the interpretation of the question. However, it is a poor excuse for bad assessment technique that the pupils will make allowances for it. And there is always the possibility that an individual candidate will be either less clever than average in reading the teacher's mind or cleverer in positing unexpected answers for poorly worded questions.

In formulating essay-type questions for assessment purposes the teacher is advised to observe these guidelines:

a) Try to compose questions which test specific skills which are required of the course the pupils have been following.
b) Phrase each question so that the candidate's task is clearly defined.
c) Avoid if possible the use of optional questions. Although these are popular with students, the practice deprives the assessor of a common basis for his evaluation. In other words it can result in different pupils taking different examinations.

Marking essays for assessment

When a teacher marks an essay assignment as a formative exercise, he does so in order to help and encourage the pupil, the learner. Some advice on how this may be done has been given in Part 1 of this book. The main principle is that every essay should be assessed individually. A teacher could quite validly speak kindly of an inferior piece of work produced by a dull pupil and be much less lenient about a better essay by a clever but lazy pupil. In marking essays for *summative* assessment purposes a teacher has to be both more circumspect and more rigid. All the essays in one exercise should be graded according to a common standard. But if there is one thing difficult to find in many essays it is common ground on which to base a standard. The commonest feature tends to be the factual knowledge displayed, and this is not the most important item in an essay-type assessment. Comparison is nowhere so odious as in creative work of the essay type, and yet the teacher has to decide how he can measure one pupil's organizational ability against another's imaginative insight.

There are two basic ways of marking history essays.

a) By grading That is to say , by dividing the essays according to a generalized norm into three or four or five grades. This type of assessment is much less difficult than it seems, and most teachers only have problems when they are asked to justify the decision that allotted Jones to Grade 5 rather than to Grade 4. If a teacher tries to express the norms he has been using in grading essays, he will probably arrive at something like the 'Southampton Scale' devised by Martin Booth (*History betrayed,* Longmans, 1969).

'Responses which showed:

1   Powers of selection, of critical thinking, and above all the ability to work relevantly outside the given material but within an historical framework were assigned to category H (= historical understanding);
2   Comprehension and intelligent handling of the material but which made little or no attempt to draw on historical material or understandings outside the question were assigned to category PC (= précis comprehension);
3   little real comprehension of the material or question and which made no attempt to expand or apply any information given were assigned to category PNC (= précis non-comprehension).'

This sort of justification of the grading system depends very much on the function of the assessment, in the case of Martin Booth's scale a research assignment. It is possible of course to transfer such grading to a numerical system, and Booth does show how his grading can be converted to a five-point or a nine-point scale.

b) By marking If the skills to be assessed by an essay are categorized satisfactorily, then it is possible to grade essays by giving a mark or marks to those aspects of the response which provide evidence of the desired skills. It is impractical for a marker to expect to be able to check more than four or five such aspects, and the marking scheme should therefore be limited to four or five possible marks, to be added for the total score of the essay. Some teachers feel they should have an unspecified reserve mark to reward unexpected but praiseworthy behaviour as well. It is important however that the scheme be made clear and easy to operate, and therefore the range of possible scores should be strictly limited. So a marking scheme might be shown as follows:

	poor	fair	good
organization/logic	1	2	3
use of evidence	1	2	3
correct use of facts	1	2	3

Here the highest possible mark for the essay is nine, and a teacher could reserve the right to allot a tenth mark for exceptional performance. The test of a satisfactory marking scheme is:

a) that is discriminates well (it distinguishes numerically between good, bad and middling performance);

b) that it discriminates on the basis of the objectives of the test: the skills which are being evaluated in the assessment.

The greatest impediment to satisfactory marking of essays, whatever the method used, is the desire or the need to get it done quickly. Essays can be marked rapidly if 'facts' only are scored. But if organization has to be assessed then the marker has to read more carefully. An examination essay should be read at the same speed and with the same care as if it were to be handed back to the writer with the teacher's comments.

Specifying the objectives to be used
in history assessment

In the first part of this chapter we quoted Norman Gronlund as asserting that the basic steps in a pupil evaluation exercise are:

1 to identify and define the objectives of instruction;

2 to construct or select forms of assessment which would appraise those specified objectives.

It is obvious that the second step depends on the first; a teacher's attempts to evaluate skills will largely depend on his ability to identify and define them.

One way of determining the means of assessment, or even in particular the types of test question which a teacher is going to set, is to construct a *table of specifications*, using a two-way chart with the course objectives on one line and the topics covered by the syllabus in the other. Figure 12 shows an example of such a table for a term's work on twentieth-century Russia. By matching objectives with content the teacher can see which sort of assessment procedure is going to be suitable. He can also use the same table for weighting the marks in an examination, since it is easy to see how the most important parts of the examination are going to be those which relate to the most vital objectives. Thus in the table given in Figure 12, we have put the mark weightings for exam questions as percentages of the total score for the examination.

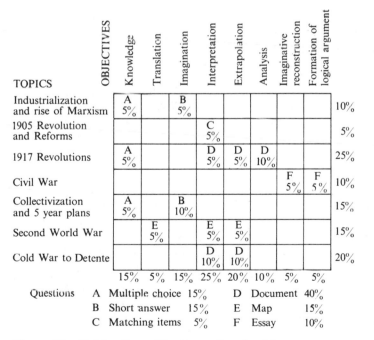

TOPICS	Knowledge	Translation	Imagination	Interpretation	Extrapolation	Analysis	Imaginative reconstruction	Formation of logical argument	
Industrialization and rise of Marxism	A 5%		B 5%						10%
1905 Revolution and Reforms				C 5%					5%
1917 Revolutions	A 5%			D 5%	D 5%	D 10%			25%
Civil War							F 5%	F 5%	10%
Collectivization and 5 year plans	A 5%		B 10%						15%
Second World War		E 5%		E 5%	E 5%				15%
Cold War to Detente				D 10%	D 10%				20%
Questions	15%	5%	15%	25%	20%	10%	5%	5%	

Questions	A	Multiple choice	15%	D	Document 40%
	B	Short answer	15%	E	Map 15%
	C	Matching items	5%	F	Essay 10%

Figure 12   Table of specifications: Russian history

Exercises

1 Using the content material of a history course for the middle years of secondary school, construct one example of each of the following test items:
short answer;
alternative response;
matching (other than time-line);
time-line;
multiple choice.

2 Using graphic or statistical material design an interpretative test for the senior secondary school syllabus.

3 In practice teaching, set an essay assignment designed to elicit performance in specified skills. Draw up a marking scheme and mark the returned essays as if for a test. If the marking does not (a) discriminate satisfactorily, or (b) give enough credit for the most important objectives, re-mark with a revised scheme.

Further reading

Denis Baron and Harold W. Bernard, *Evaluation techniques for classroom teachers,* McGraw-Hill (London, 1958).

Incorporated Association of Assistant Masters in Secondary Schools, *The teaching of history,* third edition, Cambridge University Press (London, 1965).

M.B. Booth, *History betrayed,* Longmans (London, 1969).

H.G. Macintosh and R.B. Morrison, *Objective testing,* University of London Press (London, 1969).

Benjamin S. Bloom, J. Thomas Hastings and George F. Madaus (eds.), *Handbook of formative and summative evaluation of student learning*, McGraw-Hill (New York, 1971).

Norman E. Gronlund, *Measurement and evaluation in teaching,* second edition, Macmillan (New York, 1971).

12

Public examinations and the school history syllabus

The first thing one might expect a teacher to think of when he is faced with the responsibility of teaching a class is what syllabus should be taught. Yet in this book the syllabus has been left to the very last chapter, and moreover it is linked to a discussion of the examination system. There are good reasons for this. Firstly, the syllabus, that is to say the content of the course and its general organization, must depend to a very large extent on what has already been discussed: what we think 'history' is, what its importance is in secondary education, and how many varieties there are both of teaching it and evaluating the effectiveness of that teaching. With clear ideas of *why* and *how*, we are better equipped to consider *what*. Secondly, in many countries where history is a secondary school subject, much if not all of the syllabus is determined by decisions which relate more to the public examination system than to the principles of history teaching. This is the backwash effect of examining procedures, and it would be unrealistic to consider the types of ideal syllabus a teacher might like to initiate without taking into serious consideration the effect of this backwash on his hopes and plans.

Obviously it is not desirable that all history syllabuses should take their starting point from a terminal examination. This has unfortunately happened in many instances, and the General Certificate of Education, for example, has created the pattern not only for history teaching in the year or two preceding it, but in earlier years as well, which are used to bring the pupils to the stage at which they can begin direct study for the certification exam. This has had many harmful effects on teaching in secondary schools, not only because the content of teaching has been decided by an outside (sometimes foreign) body with no contact with the human beings who are being taught or the environment in which they live and are being prepared to live, but also because most examination systems are badly run and do not provide the teacher with a clear rationale or set of general objectives upon which examinations will be set and courses can be built. If there is to be a certification exercise in history, its format should *follow* the syllabus, not determine it. This means that we should be able first to decide what is going to be taught (using the methods suggested earlier in this book) and then select that part of what is taught to be evaluated for certification. We can then make realistic decisions as to whether, for example, we want to evaluate just the final year's work or that of two, three, or more years. And there is less chance that the content of the final year will decide what is taught in earlier years.

This said, we will now follow our own advice and examine the problems of syllabus construction, and afterwards return to the problems of certification, and external and public examinations.

Constructing a syllabus

Some general principles

When a teacher sets about designing a syllabus rather than a single course, he is likely to be influenced by considerations outside the realm of history and history teaching. Is the syllabus to be designed for early school leavers or for those who stay on at school and attempt to gain admittance to further education? Or is it intended for both groups? And if it is for both groups, then which group should dominate in the 'philosophy' of the syllabus? The history teacher, like other teachers, works within an educational system. His role in that system is not only related to his subject speciality, but to the understanding of the function of a teacher in that society. Does the community expect him to prepare pupils for life in the *status quo,* or do they expect him to do something about changing it? And what does the teacher feel his relation to the community should be? Is he merely its servant, or can he as a citizen with responsibilities use his teaching role judiciously to help some of the ideas his countrymen accept? Every teacher has to ask himself this type of question, and it is only in the most totalitarian of states that there will be a very clear answer. To some extent therefore the teacher has to define not only his society's understanding of the teacher's role, but also his own interpretation of that understanding. In all these considerations of course the teacher is aware that his main concern is people, those whom he teaches as well as those by whom he is paid.

Objectives of the syllabus
The community may provide the teacher with a set of clear guidelines, or may provide him with next to nothing, but it is in the light of the opinion the teacher forms of the community needs that he draws up both his objectives and his major content. In preceding chapters we have considered instructional objectives as they relate to a course or a lesson. But they need to be worked out for a whole syllabus too. And indeed the same considerations operate and a similar list will be produced. For the sequence of learning in history is likely to be cyclical rather than linear. That is to say, while pupils of French are taken through graded exercises, each leading to a further advance in control of the language, the history student is given a variety of exercises moving continuously around the sequence of comprehension, analysis, reconstruction, and synthesis. At different stages the comprehension may be more imaginative than abstract, and the line of development leads to the defining of abstractions and the growth of a symbolic understanding, But the advance is like that of a winding staircase, hopefully spiralling upwards.

The teacher has to determine what sort of achievements he wants from his pupils at various stages in the syllabus. When should they be able to write their own notes? When should they be able to write formal essays? Study skills in which there is a linear development can be clearly defined, while the skills of historical understanding cannot. This should not lead the teacher to base his syllabus only on content and study skills, and leave out the development of historical understanding.

Content in the syllabus

The decisions about what is to be taught also depend to a large
extent upon the needs of the community. Most societies demand
that their youth should know something of their own community
history, and no matter how chauvinistic that requirement may seem
to the teacher, it has to be met. Indian secondary school leavers
who had not studied the history of the sub-continent after the
establishment of the Mughal dynasty in the sixteenth century
would be considered, and no doubt would consider themselves,
badly prepared for many of the duties of citizenship and commerce
which the community would expect them to perform. So there must
be a large element of local, regional, and national history in the
syllabus, and a fair amount of modern, contemporary history.
But this may be placed at the end of the syllabus with the certificate
candidates in mind, or in the middle, with the early leavers'
interests paramount, and outside this core there is room for
manoeuvre and choice.

We cannot possibly teach the whole of history, and selection is
usually a matter of leaving out rather than putting in. If the core
consists of national history, there are two forces pulling the teacher
towards other areas of investigation: the immediately local, with its
utilization of all the resources within the community around the
school; and the wider world—the region, the continent, the hemi-
sphere, or even general world history. Many teachers will want to
include a little of both, and should decide whether to start on a
small scale and lead pupils through local history to national and
then international affairs, or to give a 'world outlook' early in
the syllabus and narrow the range until the seniors are studying
local history in terms of political, economic, and social concepts,
and in terms of the wider scene to which they have been introduced
previously.

If the educational system leaves a large part of this decision-
making to the teacher, what principles will guide his choice? The
resources available will obviously affect this considerably. These
resources include the school library and the surrounding area.
Pupils in a brand new town in Canada or Australia may perhaps
find local history studies less interesting than inhabitants of
London or Delhi. The pupils' wishes can be consulted—if not in the
over-all organization of the programme—at least in determining

some of its details. The teacher's own interests have a place too. He is to be the historian of this subject matter, who introduces his pupils both to the topics and to his own enthusiasm for the discipline. It is therefore quite in order for him to select on the basis of his own expertise and professional interest. Very often, however, more than one teacher is involved in teaching a syllabus, in which case the interests of all concerned should be consulted. Other factors to be considered include the amount of time which is available for the mounting of the syllabus and its relation to other courses in the school programme. The history teacher needs to be aware of the progression of learning planned, for instance, in both English and geography in order to be able to phase properly the writing and cartographic skills of history, and the sequence of skill can influence the type of content a teacher chooses, or at least the order in which that content is presented.

Organization of content
When a teacher has made up his mind about what is going into the history syllabus, he has then to decide how it is to be studied: not how the individual lessons are organized, but how the narrative of history is approached. There are four main ways of organizing content in history classes, although of course combinations of these methods can lead to other interesting categories.

The chronological approach To start from the earliest topic in the list and work through chronologically until one reaches the most recent: this has perhaps been the most common way of organizing history content in secondary schools for half a century. It has two advantages: it helps the pupil to develop an understanding of the passage of time through the changing fortunes of peoples and their societies. It helps therefore to develop part of what can be called a 'time sense'. For the teacher it is undoubtedly easy. Most of the standard textbooks take the chronological approach. It makes no special demands on the organizing ingenuity of the instructor. But it has been found, over the past half-century, to have certain disadvantages:

a) A purely chronological approach leads to a scattering of concepts and themes throughout the syllabus, with very little opportunity to show the development of these themes.

b) A purely chronological approach often results in a sequence which does not take into account the psychology of pupils at different ages and stages of growth. Thus the Reformation, which requires the ability to think in a very abstract manner, is taught rather early in the secondary school if a chronological approach to European history is followed.

c) While an evolutionary approach to history is suitable for 'contemporary topics'—i.e. those of the last hundred years—it is obviously less desirable for earlier history. The need to see history 'in the round', not just a stage in the evolution of the present is regarded as desirable by most teachers of history. But development in time is a basic concept in history, and chronology must be considered in any syllabus.

Line of development approach If a purely chronological approach is not acceptable, then a chronological study of certain well defined themes may help to overcome most objections. For instance, the development of transport in almost any area of the world may provide an interesting historical topic. The development of political organization could be another such theme, and because it is only *one* theme among many it will cease to dominate the content as it does in many chronological syllabuses. This system of organization allows the teacher to introduce social and economic history to counterbalance the heavy political and military slant of much history teaching. The line of development approach certainly tends to see history in terms of evolution towards the present day. This has one advantage for the pupils; they can relate the past to the present, because the theme, before being studied in its historical aspect, can be seen in its current reality. So teachers tend to choose themes like transport or dress or towns, rather than for instance the development of alchemy, a theme which did have a vital existence in Arab and European history, but which died away, and leaves scarcely any traces in our present society. But for the growth of historical understanding this approach can be misleading. Alchemy was important in the Middle Ages. If we want simply to understand the Middle Ages as they relate to our present lives we can quite justifiably leave it out. If we want to understand the Middle

Ages 'as they were', alchemy must find a place somewhere. So the evolutionary aspect of this system of organization is historically weak unless it is modified by an occasional attempt to see an historical period 'in the round'.

The era (or patch) approach   Since it is impossible to know everything about every period that may appear in a chronologically organized syllabus, one solution is to select certain periods and study them in great detail, trying to see how the people of that time lived socially, economically, politically, and culturally. We cannot study the whole of the period from A.D. 800 to A.D. 1500 so we have to select. In Europe we would perhaps choose twelfth-century Paris and fourteenth-century Florence; in Africa, thirteenth-century Kilwa and fifteenth-century Songhai. Each period is studied in depth and an attempt is made to study from the point of view of the past rather than from a modern standpoint. Within each period the chronological development is clear, but little or no attempt is made to continue the chronological study into succeeding periods. This system enables children to explore and do project work, it offers a variety of historical aspects to be studied, and it will generally give them the 'feel' of an age which is part of the imaginative content of history as a subject. The teacher should decide for himself whether the study of a particular patch or period within the philosophy of his own syllabus is justifiable.

The comparative theme approach   One way of linking patches is to compare them, and since it is hard to compare the way a serf lived in the twelfth century with the way a peasant lived in the sixteenth, then recurrent themes should be found which can be compared in the different periods in which they recur. One might for instance study for a term various 'revolutions' either taking the word in its broadest sense (and including the Reformation, the American War of Independence, the Industrial and French Revolutions) or perhaps limiting it to social unrest, mediaeval peasants' risings and *jacqueries* through the periods of agricultural and industrial development, while another theme might look at nationalism from Joan of Arc to the most recent independence struggles in Africa. In one sense this system is related to the social sciences and helps to establish certain concepts by studying their

183

historical realizations. But it is also an historical method if each theme is related historically to the period in which it is being studied. So Wat Tyler's rebellion will be seen as a phenomenon of fourteenth-century England and the Parisian revolts of 1789 as a product of the political and economic reality in France at that time. An understanding of what 'revolution' means will emerge from the historical evidence rather than be read into it.

History in an integrated syllabus

Most of what has so far been said has rested on the assumption that the history teacher is preparing a one-subject syllabus. But many history teachers find themselves involved in integrated programmes of 'social studies', 'humanities', or even in courses which attempt to bridge the gap between the arts and the sciences. It is accepted by most history teachers nowadays that contributing to such programmes need not mean abandoning the main objects of the discipline of history so much as using those objects for a wider aim. So when an historian is asked to contribute an historical dimension to integrated studies, he has to make the same sort of decisions as he has made about his own single-subject programmes: What are the general principles of this syllabus? What content is called for? How can it be organized?

What can history offer to integrated programmes in arts or 'bridge' courses? Since many such programmes involve the study of the present environment or current society, history can offer a valuable area of contrast and comparison. Jerome Bruner made the point that to many children the study of their own surroundings can become a great bore. Only if their imaginations are stretched by use of contrast material will they retain an interest in a subject and derive intellectual benefit from it. Bruner rejected history for this role in favour of social anthropology because history in modern times covers such a wide field. But historians and especially teachers of history do not think that extent is the most important feature of their subject. No matter how chronological our studies are in organization, they never in fact do more than examine 'patches' even in our national history. The importance of history is not to create a complete picture of the past but to enable children to use evidence to create a picture, however partial, in their imaginations.

So history can help pupils to free themselves from the present and to live imaginatively in another place, another time, or another culture. Other disciplines can also contribute to this broadening of a pupil's imaginative experience. Besides social anthropology there is the more traditional field of human geography. But history has its own dimension to offer: change through time. And its role in an integrated programme should be to develop the contrasting aspects of accepted themes as they are examined in their past. As the Schools Council booklet, *Humanities and the young school leaver: an approach through history* points out (see 'Further reading' section), social or cultural themes can be studied in their present reality and in their appearances in past ages and in other societies. This involves the comparative theme approach described above which is obviously relevant to integrated programmes in any field. The assumption should be avoided that history merely offers to integrated studies a body of factual knowledge about the antecedents of any theme being examined in the present. What is much more valuable is the intellectual and imaginative exercise of searching for and recreating those 'facts' through the methods available to the classroom historian.

The history syllabus and the examinations

One important aspect of curriculum planning that a teacher has to bear in mind is who is going to assess the results of the syllabus in an examination. If the teacher himself is responsible for the testing, then he is free to teach his courses and design his assessment in the ways suggested in the previous chapter of this book. If however his pupils are to sit an external examination in the subject, then the teacher must ensure that what he teaches will give his pupils a good chance of passing. They cannot have more than a chance because the determination of their standard is out of the hands of the classroom teacher and, once they have written their examination, out of the hands of the pupils too. Unfortunately, many of the bodies responsible for external examining do not give the teacher much help in establishing just what will be examined, and what must therefore be included in the syllabus. Although they specify more or less clearly a body of content to be covered, they rarely attempt to spell out the level of mastery which is required and the specific historical and other skills without which a pupil will be judged to have failed.

Academic assessment

The more academic examinations are particularly bad in this respect, perhaps because they have hitherto been dominated by university entry requirements. In many countries secondary school certification is connected with university teaching in two ways. Firstly, the boards controlling the examinations have often either been established by universities or dominated by university representation, and secondly, the examination has for so long served as an entrance test for university places that the requirements of selection have often superseded those of certification. In his book *School examinations* John Pearce (see 'Further reading' section) has specified some of the characteristics of the British examining boards which have become models for examination councils in many parts of the developing world. The General Certificate of Education, he maintains,

began as a Victorian device and retains the basic Victorian feature that the examiners are gentlemen, working in their studies at home for a modest recognition.

He compares the British boards unfavourably with the more professional American 'Educational Testing Service', although that service has its own critic in the author of *The tyranny of testing* (see 'Further reading' section). But Pearce certainly seems correct in attributing the disinclination of boards to mount realistic pre-testing experiments in new methods of assessment to the financial restraints which arise largely from the historical division of the British examining bodies into a number of autonomous national rather than regional establishments. Pearce moreover does for the history teacher what the examining boards do not attempt, he gives an accurate description of what Ordinary level history is all about. 'In its conventional form', the history examination

involves a display of factual knowledge, retrievable at high speed in prose of great density, relating to an extensive period.

186

The three-hour essay paper has been for a long time the standard examining procedure of GCE history and much of the time and money of the history boards is spent in ensuring that this highly subjective exercise is examined in as objective and standardized a manner as possible. Some boards have experimented with interpretative questions, and a London experiment showed that such questions can discriminate as well, and provide as good an assessment, as the more traditional essay. It is to be hoped that external examining boards will begin to treat assessment more along the lines suggested in the previous chapter of this book, and history teachers who feel that such a development would be in their interest can contribute very effectively by joining such boards as examiners, assessors, and members of whatever committees are used for advisory purposes.

But what is the teacher to do with the traditional examination while it lasts? He cannot of course ignore it. He must teach for it and enable as many of his pupils to pass it as possible. But he can do that in a way that is both intelligent and selective. Most boards offer a variety of papers and the teacher will find that any of the four means of organizing the syllabus given above can be used to suit the content of at least one paper. In teaching the course the methods of instruction described in the first part of this book will provide a thorough training not only in the skills of the subject (which are probably not going to be examined) but in the content as well. What the teacher has to determine is (a) how long he is going to spend on the content matter of the examinations as such, and (b) when and how he is going to prepare pupils for the form of the exam, the half-hour essay. The length of papers differs from board to board, and no general rule can be applied in answering the first question. For many papers, four terms are ample, and experienced teachers should be able to prepare pupils sufficiently in three terms or the final year. For other systems and in other environments more time, perhaps two years, may be required. Such is the case in many developing countries where the medium of instruction is a second language and where the Cambridge overseas syllabuses tend to be very long. The length of time spent on the syllabus content will also determine how long is devoted to the only 'skill' required. Formal essays should be written frequently during the last year of preparation for the examination, and should be supported by a thorough grounding in note-making skills at an earlier stage. Since map-work has for some time been a feature of these examinations, exercise in that area too must be included in the work of the 'certificate year'.

Non-academic assessment

Besides university-dominated academic examinations, other types of public examination are taken by secondary school leavers. In some countries these are 'junior secondary certificates' given after the second or third year of secondary schooling. In Britain there is the Certificate of Secondary Education which may be taken as an alternative to the GCE by those who leave school at the statutory age of sixteen. Both these types of examination have one feature in common: they are intended mainly as certification for the less academic members of the school population. It follows therefore that the objectives both of the syllabus they follow and the examination which assesses their achievement are related to their lives as citizens and their contribution to their own and the community's development. Just how those aims are defined differs from community to community. But it is important that the less academic syllabus, where there is one, has its own rationale and should not be designed as a watered-down version of the GCE.

The less academic forms of certification are not usually as much dominated by university involvement as the academic examinations. Examining bodies are frequently set up by Ministries or Departments of Education for junior secondary certification, and the CSE in Britain is examined by regional bodies on which there is always a majority of serving teachers. In Britain, according to Pearce, this system has resulted in a much more professional approach to examining, because the assessors and moderators employed by the Regional Boards are trained in their tasks, while the GCE examiners are still amateurs in the Victorian tradition. Whether it is the Ministry or some other body that determines the format of the less academic examination, there is usually much greater scope for serving teacher involvement than there is with university-dominated bodies. Regionalism, as embodied in the CSE structure, also has its advantages, especially for history. While GCE boards are national or even multinational in their interests (the overseas Cambridge board has been replaced by multinational bodies like the West African and East African certificate boards), the history teacher would often like his pupils to investigate the riches of their own immediate environment. The regionalism of the CSE permits this to a much larger extent than does a national body.

Teacher-assessed public examinations

Local history can never be an examinable part of the syllabus if the local teacher is not free to determine at least part of the assessment for himself. In the British CSE and in some GCE systems this is a possibility. Besides the exams assessed by a completely external body of examiners, and of a body with strong teacher representation, there are those in which part of the examination is set and marked by the class teacher, even if moderated externally. At the less academic level, this has been frequently practised for the CSE, and even at the Ordinary level of the GCE interesting examples of Mode Three examining have been published. In one school, for example, the 'O' level examination consists of three sections. One is a nationally set paper from the examining body, the other two are forms invented by the class teacher: a project which counted for 66% of the local contribution and an essay written under examination conditions but with the help of notes from the project, which counted for 33%.

Evidently it is either the teacher who feels that his syllabus has so much to offer the pupils that it should not make way for that of the public examination, or even more rarely the teacher who feels that his form of assessment is better than the norm, who will apply to the examining authority for permission to set a 'Mode Three' paper. This application has to be submitted at least eighteen months and often more before the examination is due to take place, for the permission of the board needs to be obtained before the course to be examined is begun. And since the manner of application differs from authority to authority, the teacher should become acquainted with the regulations of the board to which he will make his submission as soon as possible.

Certification or selection:
the problem for secondary school history

The Mode Three type of public assessment in Britain seems to indicate a move away from external examining altogether towards a form of school examination externally moderated for public recognition. This appears to be similar to the system practised in the United States of America, where 'graduation' from the high school is determined by the school system itself, and admission to further education is determined by the selecting body making use of high school placings, course hours accredited, grade records of the whole high school career and the results of an externally administered Scholastic Aptitude Test. What prevails in the United States therefore is a certification system in the schools which the universities or other institutes of higher education are free to use or not in their own processes of selecting candidates.

The effects of the basic choice between a selection examination (and a syllabus geared towards it) and a certification procedure may be important to the secondary school history teacher. Not only does the Certificate of Secondary Education provide a teacher with a greater freedom in deciding what will be assessed and how; it also obliges him to think of his subject as it affects the cognitive and affective growth of the adolescent in school, rather than as it relates to future courses in higher education. There is a danger that all secondary teachers who have themselves passed through school into college will think of their schooldays as a prelude to the really academic stuff of the degree or training course. For the history teacher this danger is all the greater. His subject is not one that requires a clear sequence of knowledge and skill. It is not one which has been adequately defined even at an academic level. Outsiders have accused it of having no clear method and of contributing no discrete form of knowledge. And yet the teacher knows that he has in some way been 'formed' to an historical mode of thinking by his studies, especially his tertiary studies. It is too easy to regard secondary school history therefore as a preparation for 'real history' at college or university.

This book has attempted to persuade the future teacher of history to look a little harder at his chosen *métier*, to think out his attitude to the subject and his place as an educator in the intellectual growth of secondary school adolescents. History to the historian is not merely an intellectual activity; it is an enjoyable, fascinating, and often an enthralling activity. Whatever methods a teacher chooses, whatever types of syllabus he selects, he should bring with him that attitude which not even the prospect of externally judged examinations should dim. A teacher does not teach for the sake of certification, even though he is professionally obliged to certify as a result of his teaching. But certification and the assessment which leads to it is only a small part of his task. The teacher who has not succeeded in leading a large proportion of his pupils to an enjoyment of the discovery of the past will feel that he has failed, no matter how well his pupils do in external examinations. And the teacher should be in no doubt about where the core of the joy of history can be found. It is not in the method, not in the fact that it investigates the past, not in the fact that it is primarily an act of the imagination, but because it is wholly the study of people. As Marc Bloch explained:

Behind the features of landscape, behind tools or machinery, behind what appear to be the most formalized written documents, and behind institutions which seem almost entirely detached from their founders, there are men, and it is men that history seeks to grasp.

Further reading

M.V.C. Jeffreys, *History in the schools: the study of development,* Pitman (London, 1939).

W.H. Burston, 'The history teacher and the GCE' in W.H. Burston and C.W. Green, *Handbook for history teachers*, second edition, Methuen (London, 1972).

P. Carpenter, *History teaching: the era approach,* Cambridge University Press (London, 1964).

Banesh Hoffmann, *The tyranny of testing,* Collier (New York, 1964).

Schools Council, *The Certificate of Secondary Education: the place of the personal topic. History,* HMSO (London, 1968).

Schools Council, *Humanities for the young school leaver: an approach through history,* Evans-Methuen (London, 1969).

Henry G. Macintosh, 'Assessment in "O" level history', in *Teaching History,* vol. II, No. 5 (1971).

W.H. Burston, 'The syllabus in the secondary school' in W.H. Burston and C.W. Green, *Handbook for history teachers,* second edition, Methuen (London, 1972).

R. Ben Jones, 'Oakham School Mode III history "O" level', in *Teaching History,* vol. II, No. 7 (1972).

John Pearce, *School examinations,* Collier-Macmillan (London, 1972).

Carolyn M. Ferguson and Sean Garrett, 'Stimulus material in "O" level history', in *Educational Research,* vol. 17, No. 2 (1973).